T0209640

TEACHER EVALUATION
AS A
GROWTH PROCESS

Dianna Whitlock, Ed.D.

authorHOUSE®

AuthorHouse™
1663 Liberty Drive
Bloomington, IN 47403
www.authorhouse.com
Phone: 1 (800) 839-8640

Published by AuthorHouse 05/15/2020

ISBN: 978-1-7283-6140-6 (sc)
ISBN: 978-1-7283-6139-0 (e)

Library of Congress Control Number: 2020908822

Print information available on the last page.

ACKNOWLEDGEMENTS

I would like to thank Standard For Success for their support and collaboration in this project. Specific thanks to the founders Alan Degener, Todd Whitlock, and Robbie Grimes for their cooperation. Thank you also to friends, family, and colleagues who offered support and encouragement during this project.

FOREWORD

I have read numerous books and journals on the evaluation process, but none capture the "why" like Dianna Whitlock does in this book. When the majority of teachers hear the word "evaluation", it sends shivers down their spine and beads of sweat to their forehead. The thought of having yet another principal from a revolving door of endless principals that have come and gone enter their classroom and observe, question, critique, and even scrutinize their instruction based on that particular individual's assumption of what he or she thinks is "effective instruction" can be daunting and even demoralizing for any teacher. These annual acts of subjectivity often leave even the most veteran teachers frustrated and discouraged. When I was a teacher, I would often hear new teachers asking veteran teachers, "what is it that the principal is looking for in the observation", or "how should I teach this lesson to get scored as highly effective?". We cannot blame teachers for their role in the "dog and pony show" when they are observed by their administrator, as they are merely trying to stay afloat in what seems to be a sea of new principals with varying opinions on what quality instruction should look like. Dr. Whitlock does a wonderful job of deconstructing the evaluation process and in doing so, shows us the benefits of the evaluation process, as it is the very foundation to provide clarity and consistency within the organization.

When educators know exactly what is expected of them and they are familiar with the rubric used to evaluate their performance, the nerve racking subjectivity of trying to guess what their principal is looking for is replaced with the agreed upon essential components of effective instructional practices that are expected in any classroom, in every school within the district.

Dr. Whitlock's view of providing teachers with quality feedback is spot on! I strongly recommend this book to all administrators and aspiring administrators, because far too many have been led to believe that teacher evaluations are meant to be "gotcha moments", instead of opportunities for growth, as Whitlock states in her book. This book is a refreshing reminder of how important it is to be an effective communicator, and that level of clarity can only be fostered and sustained through clear expectations and a shared understanding that result from a solid evaluation framework. This book is an amazing resource for all administrators and I firmly believe it should be a required reading in all administrative certification programs.

Thomas J. Colabufo, Superintendent
Central Square School District
Central Square, New York

PART I

CHAPTER 1

PURPOSE OF BOOK

"What gets measured gets done."
(Drucker, 1954)

The above quote may be to many the cornerstone around which employee evaluation has evolved. Without a system of measurement in the workplace, would employees complete tasks? More importantly, would they continue to grow and evolve in their current roles?

Immediately, we get a variety of answers, as some state the importance of allowing teachers to teach, and not giving them one more *hoop* through which to jump or task to complete. Administrators and human resource directors may argue that without a system to measure employee performance, there may be little motivation for those in their employ to strive for improvement. Further, Robert Greenleaf and his theories on servant leadership would tell us that true employee growth occurs when those in our employee are having their needs recognized and met (Greenleaf, 2002). Therefore, are we looking for a better metric of measurement, or a better way of gauging and meeting the needs of our employees?

The answer is both and neither, collectively. We must both meet the needs of our employees and find the best way to measure their productivity. However, neither of these can exist without first and foremost building a culture of feedback in our organizations. A complete structure of consistent, timely feedback is essential to any system of employee evaluation, regardless of the metric being used to measure performance (Darling-Hammond, Amrein-Beardsley, Haertel, & Rothstein, 2012).

In this book, we are focusing on the evaluation of educators. While we tend to think of this as a *teacher evaluation* book, there are also theories and concepts in this book that encompass the other educators in our organizations, such as principals, superintendents, etc. In addition, many of the specifics of this book are applicable to non-certified or classified personnel such as custodians, instructional assistants, secretaries, bus drivers, etc. A third application of this book could be performance evaluation of any employees in any organization. While we are focusing primarily on educators, there are applications for others in an evaluative role within a company.

It is important to recognize the evaluation process as just that—a process. Therefore, this is not a how to book, with a step by step list of how to best implement the teacher evaluation system in your school. This is true for two reasons. The first is that an organization must be measuring the behaviors and actions that they value. This is discussed further in Chapter Four on choosing and defining rubrics for teacher performance. The second is that again, the process must remain a process. True growth and improvement happen when the organization is fostering and supporting individual growth of employees based on collected evaluation data.

As a lifelong educator, I believe that it is within all of us to want to do well. While this statement is subjective, we must remember that the desire to improve, especially among those working in service professions such as teaching, is fundamental. Employees who feel that their input and service is valued are more likely to strive for improvement of performance.

As educational leaders, we must ensure that feedback is meaningful, not only for individual employee improvement, but for the success of our schools as a whole. Are we analyzing trend evaluation data to drive professional development? Are we analyzing evaluator data to ensure that they are consistently providing appropriate feedback? When these criteria are met, we increase our chances of providing meaningful, intrinsic feedback for teachers and ultimately improving schools for our students.

CHAPTER 2

WHY EVALUATE

The beginning of many educators' careers saw little consistency in the teacher evaluation process (Andrews, 2016, Powerpoint slide 3). Often times evaluation day would look something like this: an administrator (likely the principal) would tell a beginning teacher that they would stop by for an observation sometime that week. The teacher would then prepare many visuals and engaging activities for the upcoming lesson, so the students would be responsive and involved. After a showboat lesson, the administrator would leave a post-it note on the teacher's desk saying something like, *Enjoyed the lesson, keep up the good work!* The administrator would then complete a checklist for the teacher, place a copy in their mailbox, and the teacher would sign and return it. This would likely be the last interaction concerning evaluation for the year.

As an elementary teacher, I was guilty of saving my best lessons for evaluation week. These lessons usually involved candy or cereal of some kind to be used as manipulatives. The reasons for this are fairly obvious. The kids were excited, the activities were endless: graphing, sorting, adding, subtracting, etc., and the best overarching bribe of all, *If you do a good job and complete all of the activities, you can eat them at the end of the lesson.* The idea here being that if it was a super-fun, hands-on lesson where kids were engaged (or maybe just hungry), you could wow your administrator and likely not suffer an observation for another year.

While my colleagues and I agreed that the positive reinforcement that stemmed from a summary of a job well done was pleasant, true constructive

- 9:00 am: parent who has been waiting while I was talking to bus driver needs to see me immediately; her child is being bullied and she will call the local news channels if it is not stopped.
- 10:30 am: student sent to office for discipline…and so on, and so on…

Does this sound familiar? As the day wore on, I would begin questioning if I would even have a chance to eat a quick lunch at my desk, never mind getting out to visit classrooms! While time management was certainly the most obvious issue here, there was another. As an administrator, I had not set a value, or urgency, on teacher evaluation. This was in part due to my own unawareness of the importance of teacher evaluation to my school. If the teachers were doing an adequate job, and I had a multitude of other tasks to which I needed to attend, then observations often were pushed to the back burner.

We also need to explore the role of the building level administrator in the above scenario. We expect a building leader to handle the above-mentioned managerial tasks of the day to day operations of the school, as well as serve as an instructional leader and nurture the school's vision and promote student learning (ELCC standards, 2011). Each of these situations are important to the individual affected, and should be dealt with in a timely manner. It is difficult sometimes to display both of these leadership skills simultaneously.

From a veteran teacher perspective, there was not often a priority placed upon teacher evaluation. If as a teacher, I have been doing a good job, or at least a good enough job, then is there a need for evaluation? Again, this was at a time when evaluations were only used for documentation for teacher dismissal, and not for constructive feedback. Therefore, giving feedback to drive professional growth and improvement was not a familiar concept. In fact, it often caused stress to teachers, who feared that a presence from an administrator for an evaluation may mean that they were in danger of dismissal.

As well as the time factor and the lack of urgency, there is another reason that school districts often failed to establish a teacher evaluation procedure based on meaningful feedback. Over the past several decades, the focus of schools has primarily been on initiatives to improve students' standardized test scores (Gershon, 2015, para 5). There was little research to document that teacher evaluation would directly impact said scores, so therefore the time, energy, and resources were spent on instructional techniques focused on student achievement and mastery of standards. While the No Child Left Behind Initiative focused on teacher quality, there was no specific focus on teacher performance or monitoring of instructional strategies.

Perhaps the biggest reason that teacher evaluations were not given the time and attention in the past that they have in recent years is that traditionally, evaluations lacked validity and alignment with professional standards. They also tended to seldom be comprehensive, routine, or systematic (Andrews, 2016, Powerpoint slide 6).

Around 2011, this began to change for many schools across the country. Educators and legislators were beginning to discuss teacher evaluation tied to school accountability. State departments of education were now requiring schools to report staff performance quantitatively. Administrators were now being asked to assign a numerical value to pre-determined areas of teaching using a rubric. For many school districts, this was replacing a subjective narrative format.

This was a monumental change for administrators and teachers who had for years participated in the evaluation *process* outlined in Chapter One. No more quick drop-ins to leave a post-it on the desk. No more simple narratives to be placed in the teacher's mailbox and never discussed. No more skipping teachers for years at a time, or only visiting those with whom there have been issues or questions about their instructional methods. There was now a reporting component to teacher evaluation, moving it up the scale of priorities for administrators and teachers.

During this change, we saw many educators begin to show signs of evaluation fatigue. This continues for some today. Since teacher evaluation was a buzz word in the early 2010's, it was believed by some that it would go through the same life cycle as many other educational initiatives. While many administrators have established a teacher evaluation system that works for their district, and are now analyzing the data to drive professional growth for teachers, others have decided to wait it out and see if this too shall pass.

This is understandable to a point, as veteran educators have witnessed a paradigm shift in most educational initiatives. To those who feel, or have felt in the past, that they have poured effort and passion into an initiative just to have it be altered or dropped the following year, skepticism is valid. However, we live in an age of accountability like no other prior. Not only is it best practice to utilize data to drive your school initiatives and teacher growth and development planning, but it is expected. We must remain as data driven for our teachers as we do for our students to make our schools better for all.

Another component of teacher evaluation in the early stages might be a nuance of *us vs. them*. Teachers may question why administrators are insisting on another *new* initiative, giving them one more thing to do. There is an outcry from teachers and their unions to just let them teach. But just as we must evaluate how our students are growing as learners, we must also evaluate how teachers are growing as practitioners.

Best practice dictates that the teacher be highly engaged in the evaluation process development, to help eliminate this *us vs. them* mentality. The most successful schools include the teachers in discussions and developments concerning teacher evaluation, from rubric creation and updates to the creation of the district evaluation plan.

When we examine educational philosophical theory, the neo-institutional theory provides support for those who include local norms and needs in developing their teacher evaluation practices. While laws and mandates often define teacher evaluation, schools do have some flexibility in how they design and implement their individual policies at the local level. This aligns with the concept of neo-institutional theory, which advocates that, "the structure of societal and political organizations exerts independent effects on policy" (Crowson, Boyd, and Mawhinney, 1996; Peters, 1999; Scott, 1995 as cited by Cooper, Fusarelli, and Randall, 2004).

While the steps of an evaluation model are important, perhaps of greater importance is the culture of the organization. Is the evaluation procedure designed to be punitive and threatening, or is it designed to provide constructive feedback to foster individual employee growth through targeted professional development? If the only goal of the teacher evaluation is employee dismissal, it stands to reason that employees will view the process negatively. We may be a little uncomfortable knowing that our performance is being observed, but we also know that our greatest growth occurs when we are outside of our comfort zones. To give the teacher an opportunity to participate in the process, through artifact contribution, conferencing, and goal setting, involves the teacher in such a manner that they now have ownership in their evaluation. In this way, teacher evaluation is being done for the teacher, and not being done to the teacher.

CHAPTER 4

RUBRICS

The use of the rubric itself is new to many involved in teacher evaluation. As we explained in previous chapters, many school districts were using narratives until recent years. Some districts may have elected to use a checklist that included a four-point scale. However, most of these did not define each indicator. For example, common checklists in the early years of teacher evaluation may have required that a teacher be rated on student engagement by asking the evaluator to check a 1, 2, 3, or 4. However, many did not define what the 1, 2, 3, or 4 looked like to the evaluator. This made the evaluation practice only slightly more objective than the narrative format. From a teacher perspective, feedback was limited, because they were not informed of the expectations required to earn a specific mark in student engagement.

A rubric, by definition is:

- an established rule, tradition, or custom or
- a guide listing specific criteria for grading or scoring academic papers, projects, or tests
  (Mirriam-Webster, 2019).

Both of these definitions can be applied when we are talking about teacher evaluation rubrics. The first definition, that which includes an established rule, is exactly what districts do when they adopt, adapt, or write a teacher evaluation rubric. They are establishing the rules by which they expect teachers to perform, improve, and excel.

When we typically think of academic rubrics, we may think of the second definition as it applies to scoring student work. However, when we evaluate a teacher based upon a pre-approved rubric, we are indeed providing feedback based upon a set of pre-determined standards. In this case, the *project* is the teacher's classroom performance.

To delve a little deeper, we can refer to the educational philosophical construct of essentialism. Supporters of essentialism believe that there is a "body of specific knowledge and absolute standards of thought" (Cooper, et al., 2004). This seems to be the basis for application of any academic standards or rubric, especially as they relate to teacher evaluation. Teacher evaluation rubrics and student academic standards set *absolutes* for performance.

In response to changes in teacher evaluation mandates and state level reporting, some states and individual districts began creating teacher rubrics. The purpose of these rubrics was to provide a uniform platform with which to evaluate teachers. Many school districts chose to adopt research-based rubrics presently available. While the rubrics discussed in this chapter are not all-inclusive, we will attempt to examine some of the most commonly used rubrics in the field of education.

It is necessary to distinguish some terminology at this point. While we have defined a rubric, it is important to note that this is only a small portion of the entire evaluation process explained in this book. Simply adopting a rubric is a single, though critical, step in this practice.

Another term that deserves definition is the teacher evaluation platform. This is the means by which school district's administrators elect to manage teacher evaluation. This may be done by utilizing a commercial software program, a spreadsheet, or paper and pencil. The terms *rubric* and *platform* are often used inter-changeably, thus creating confusion to those involved in the holistic process of teacher evaluation. For example, Standard For Success is an example of a platform that can house and manage a variety of rubrics.

A third term that we hear is *framework*, sometimes called the roadmap (Danielson, 2007). We often hear a school state that they are using a certain framework, when what they actually mean is that they are using a rubric. For purposes of this book, we define the rubric as the actual metric, and the framework as the overarching process. For example, if a school states that they are using The Thoughtful Classroom framework, they are not only using the rubric, but all recommended steps in the evaluation process such as pre and post conferences, teacher self-assessments, etc. In her book *Enhancing Professional Practice* (2007), Charlotte Danielson states, "a framework for teaching provides the structure for such discussions [professional dialogue] and an opportunity for genuine professionalism." (Danielson, 2007, p. 12).

Types of Rubrics

Danielson

Charlotte Danielson's framework for evaluating teachers attempts to represent all aspects of teaching. It is based upon the idea that if we expect students to learn at a high level, then our teachers must instruct at a high level (Danielson, 2007). It is designed to be comprehensive, based upon research, and non-specific to individual instructional strategies. The rubric itself divides teaching into domains of instructional and non-instructional areas of teaching. The Danielson framework is reflective of the work of Madeline Hunter, who described teaching as both an art and a science, and correlated instructional strategies to student achievement (Wittrock, 1986, as cited in Danielson, 2007, p. 7).

It has been noted by some that the Danielson rubric, while effectively capturing the essence of teaching practice, is missing some crucial elements of instruction such as technology and cultural diversity. However, Danielson states that these elements are not represented as the actual work of teaching, but are represented in the way in which a teacher instructs. As such, there is an assumption of equity within the framework, and all students benefit from the strong instructional strategies implemented by the teacher (Danielson, 2007). Likewise, technology is recognized as a tool with which to deliver instruction, and not an instructional strategy in its own right.

The Thoughtful Classroom

The evaluation component of Harvey Silver's Thoughtful Classroom Teacher Effectiveness Framework (TCTEF) includes observation, evaluation, and refinement of instructional practice. The philosophy of teacher evaluation within TCTEF is that not only does an evaluator look for evidence of researched-based effective instruction, but also provides the professional development and coaching by providing instructional *tools* that respond to teachers' challenges and that are most likely to improve the quality of student learning.

The TCTEF rubric is divided into three separate components. The first component, entitled *The Four Cornerstones of Effective Classrooms*, emphasizes the learning environment, including organization, rules, and procedures; positive relationships; engagement and enjoyment; and a culture of thinking and learning. The second component, *The Five Epsiodes of Effective Instruction*, allows evaluator input on the teacher's design and delivery of instruction. This encompasses how the teacher prepares students for new learning, assists students as they obtain and practice learning, and challenges students to apply learning. The third component, *Effective Professional Practice*, attends to non-instructional dimensions associated with teaching, such as leadership, professional development, and contributions to the school community (Silver Strong & Associates, 2013).

Marzano

Robert Marzano has become a leader not only in the area of teacher evaluation, but in educational research and instructional strategies (Room 241, 2012). At the cornerstone of Marzano's framework is improved classroom strategies. Teachers choose areas of improvement and administrators monitor this through observations. Feedback and dialogue are central to teacher success in the classroom (Room 241, 2012).

TAP

While some systems do not address merit or performance pay, the TAP system and rubric embeds this into their framework as teachers are paid based on their skills, knowledge, additional responsibilities, and student performance (National Institute for Excellence in Teaching, 2010). Also included in TAP is a system for periodic professional growth and development. Originally designed as a system of school reform, TAP utilizes four domains for teacher evaluation: multiple career paths, ongoing applied professional growth, instructionally focused accountability, and performance-based compensation (National Institute for Excellence in Teaching, 2010).

Under the TAP system, teachers may achieve master and mentor status and be compensated accordingly. Along with administrators, these teachers observe and evaluate their peers using a research-based rubric that is monitored by school leadership teams (National Institute for Excellence in Teaching, 2010).

State Created and Mandated Rubrics

Many of the 50 US states have a teacher evaluation rubric in place through their department of education. These may be mandated or may be available for use by school districts if they so choose. In some cases, these are allowed to be modified to meet the needs of individual districts.

In 2011, Indiana created the RISE rubric in order to support legislation on teacher evaluation. This state code "requires charter schools, including virtual charters, and school corporations to provide the disaggregated results of staff performance evaluations by teacher identification numbers to the IDOE." (Indiana Department of Education website, n.d.).

As a result, the Indiana Teacher Evaluation Cabinet created RISE. This committee of Indiana educators refined the rubric based on teacher and principal input. The system was designed to organize the evaluation into four categories to give teachers productive and timely feedback (RISE Evaluation and Development, n.d.). While this was not the only *new* rubric under discussion and consideration at the time, it was adopted by many schools to meet the new reporting and compliance mandates and adapted to meet their individual needs over time. Many states have followed suit with similar state rubrics.

Locally Created

A locally created rubric is just that, a rubric that has been created by a local district or organization. Many districts have teacher evaluation committees who meet regularly for the purpose of creating and revising an evaluation rubric to meet their district's needs. These committees usually have representation from various groups invested in teacher evaluation, such as district level administrators, building level administrators, and teachers. Input from employees and association representatives in designing an evaluation rubric can increase employee buy-in and ownership in the final product.

There is a belief among some, however, that the locally created rubric might lack research-based instructional strategies. Therefore, some schools have elected to adopt a state or commercially created rubric and adapt it to include their individual initiatives. For example, a school district may adopt the Danielson framework, but add elements to the rubric that measure goals or initiatives specific to their district. This ensures that they are on track with national norms and standards, while still evaluating norms that are valued locally.

It is best practice for administrative teams to review, revise, and improve their rubrics annually, if not more often. It is particularly helpful to have teacher representatives on these teams that review, revise, and improve their rubric language to incorporate local norms and expectations into existing rubrics to meet individual district needs. This helps foster professional growth that is more personalized and relevant to a specific school district.

CHAPTER 5

MERIT PAY

In any profession, when we begin discussions on performance ratings, we tend to automatically think of merit pay. Merit pay is typically pay based upon performance, and the model has been used in the business world for decades, specifically in the sales field. Why else would an employee be motivated to perform well, if not for financial compensation?

The conflict within the education world is that teaching has historically been viewed as a service profession. Further, teachers do not depend upon an hourly rate or base salary, but have always been paid a fixed salary to complete tasks assigned. To suggest that they could earn more or less based upon performance is a foreign concept to the veteran teacher.

There still remains a belief among many that tying teacher evaluation to merit pay will motivate teachers to increase student achievement. New research suggests that this may not be the case. While the traditional "carrot and stick" (Pink, 2011, as cited by T. Whitlock, 2015, p. 74) model of extrinsic motivation works well when there is a clear, pre-determined set of expectations and one simple solution, this is not the case for teachers. For those working with students, there is often not one single solution, rather several possibilities for an outcome. Therefore, the if-then reward systems tended to block creativity, thus limiting employee productivity (T. Whitlock, 2015).

What, then, does motivate educators to improve performance? According to Whitlock, "participation in decision making, independence and expression of creativity are all drivers for high internal motivation."

(Pink, 2011, as cited by Whitlock, 2015, p. 74). To put it in simpler terms, teachers want to be listened to. This need is more obvious than ever today with the presence of social media. It doesn't take long, while browsing Facebook, to see posts from teacher groups expressing the negatives of their profession such as low pay, long hours, and lack of support from parents. Linkedin, which is meant to maintain a more formal medium for professionals, has also become a forum for posts on the inequities of teacher pay and working conditions in comparison to other professions. These new platforms reiterate the idea that teachers seek a voice for their vocation.

There are two common concerns about merit pay in the field of education. The first is that in order to receive supplementary compensation, there must be a metric. Certainly, the teacher evaluation rubric is helpful here. Teachers and administrators still meet these changes with some resistance. Teachers who have not experienced an evaluation process built on constructive feedback fear variation to that which is familiar and being identified as the key influence on student achievement (Skourdoumbis, 2013). While student learning objectives may allow teachers to set their own goals related to student achievement, many remain concerned that outside factors, such as teacher/student relationships (Marzano, 2012), affecting student growth will not be taken into account.

The second way in which classroom teaching differs from the sales model mentioned above is that teachers have little control over the external factors affecting their students. We do, however, maintain an expectation that a highly effective teacher will go above and beyond to provide instructional and motivational strategies that will guarantee student success, in spite of these external factors, and that the overall tone set in the classroom can also contribute to this (Skourdoumbis, 2013).

There is a well-known story among educators about the perils of operating a school like a business. While some have argued that this is an economically sound method for school reform, *The Blueberry Story* (Volmer, 2011) presents a problem with this method of school reform, and is one of the best examples of the lack of control educators have over external factors in our schools. In summary, it is a story of a representative from a group of business leaders speaking to a large group of educators at a symposium. The businessman, who was an executive at an ice cream company, lectures the educators on the advantages of running schools like businesses. This includes maintaining continuous improvement, quality management, and demanding zero defects.

All seemed to be going well, until a veteran teacher asked what the man would do in his line of work if he received a crate of rotten blueberries with which to produce his famous blueberry ice cream. When he had to admit that he would send them back, the teacher reminded him that as educators, we do not have this option. We take EVERYONE! (Volmer, 2011).

This lack of control over external factors leads to a dilemma for administrators when preparing class assignments for their schools. Podgursky and Springer (2007) state concerns in their research about using value added measures in administrative decisions, especially those that may affect policies or staffing (Podgursky & Springer, 2007, as cited in Hanushek & Rivkin, 2010, p. 4). In addition, Rothstein (2008) expresses concern that if classroom assignments are not arbitrary, then inequities may exist when measuring student growth (Rothstein, 2008, as cited by David, 2010, p. 81). Therefore, if a teacher has a strength or a passion for working with students who are struggling academically, will they be penalized in the merit pay system if their students do not score well on a standardized test? Or will the teacher of the high ability students be penalized if their students do not show growth, because they have already scored as high as possible on a standardized test? If teachers are being denied compensation due to these factors, can we expect them to continue to volunteer to work with the groups of students for whom they have a passion and/or received specialized training? While no clear answers exist, the following chapter on value added measures will attempt to address some possible solutions.

CHAPTER 6

VALUE ADDED MEASURES

While Chapter Five pointed out some inconsistencies and common concerns from educators with traditional merit pay systems utilized in the business world, most educators are in favor of some form of accountability when it comes to measuring student growth. Evaluation systems typically include some type of value-added measure as part of their holistic teacher evaluation process. Many states mandate that a percentage of a teacher's final evaluation rating include a value-added measure.

Since so many systems of monitoring teacher progress must be tied to student progress, there has been much discussion on the best way to bring these two together. While evaluators can observe teacher and student traits that are classified as effective, student learning must be documented. This is usually done with student test scores, although educators are aware that many external factors affect these scores. The most effective evaluation systems are those that measure both teacher traits and student results. This is summarized well by Phi Delta Kappan:

> These tools are most effective when embedded in systems that support evaluation expertise and well- grounded decisions, by ensuring that evaluators are trained, evaluation and feedback are frequent, mentoring and professional development are available, and procedures are in place to support due process. (Darling-Hammond, Amrein-Beardsley, Haertel, & Rothstein, 2012)

test is utilized, it is essential to test for reliability and validity (Steele, Hamilton, & Stecher, 2011).

School-wide Percentages

When growth model data was first introduced, there was significant concern from teachers of the high stakes testing grades that the most pressure would be on them to demonstrate adequate student growth under this proposed system. By tying it to the school grade and student body as a whole, the accountability piece is shared among the staff and creates ownership in the method.

If the mandated test is given in grade four, then grade three teachers impact the students' education the previous year. While this creates a culture of shared responsibility, student transience and teacher turnover can disrupt the structure.

Student Learning Objectives

In order to encourage teacher input, some districts have encouraged teachers to set student learning objectives (SLO's). An SLO should contain a student goal and assessment to measure that goal (Reform Support Network, n.d.). These are often based upon SMART goals in that they are expected to be Specific, Measurable, Attainable, Realistic, and Timely. In setting SLO's, teachers determine the expected progress that will be made by students throughout the school year, using assessment data. They should align with overarching school and district goals, as well as state or national standards (Reform Support Network, n.d.).

While time consuming, teachers have greater ownership in the measure of student achievement by creating SLO's than with some other value-added measures. A 2015 study showed that teachers using student learning objectives as a measure of student growth were more likely to meet their self-specified goals than those using other value-added measures, such as test scores (USDOE, 2015). Value added measures tended to show a wider distribution of teacher effectiveness scores, represented by a bell curve. This may be due to teacher created SLO's not containing the rigor of other value-added measures. To ensure rigor, some states require approval of teacher created SLO's by their department of education.

A Missing Piece

A concern of educators, and specifically classroom teachers, is that it is difficult to evaluate teacher/student relationship and teacher influence. When working with school administrators on teacher evaluation, I often pose the following theoretical question: How do you measure the teacher/student relationship? It has been answered that this can be documented under teacher leadership, professionalism, etc. I do not disagree, as teacher/student communication is often present under these domains in teacher evaluation rubrics. In fact, Danielson rubrics include ratings for respect and rapport with students in the classroom environment domain and communication with students in the instructional domain (Danielson Group, 2013).

While classroom teachers and administrators alike have always known that there are external factors affecting student growth (remember the blueberry story from Chapter Five), the following research specifies a list. While not all inclusive, the following list from Darling-Hammond, et al. (2012) name some elements that have an impact on student achievement:

- School factors such as class sizes, curriculum materials, instructional time, availability of specialists and tutors, and resources for learning (books, computers, science labs, and more);
- Home and community supports or challenges;
- Individual student needs and abilities, health, and attendance;
- Peer culture and achievement;
- Prior teachers and schooling, as well as other current teachers;
- Differential summer learning loss, which especially affects low-income children; and
- The specific tests used, which emphasize some kinds of learning and not others and which rarely measure achievement that is well above or below grade level. (Darling-Hammond, et al., 2012, p. 8)

The research team further elaborates that value-added measures do not appropriately gauge these elements of student achievement effectively, but rather use statistical methods to quantify student growth (Darling-Hammond et al., 2012).

But there is a vaguer, more subjective element to the teacher student relationship. How does an administrator measure the teacher who just *gets* or *clicks with* a student? We have all known the student that has struggled since kindergarten, possibly they have been our daily office referral. Then in third grade, that same student finds his comfort zone, perhaps because of a connection with the teacher. How can this be measured on a rubric?

This more personal element of the teacher student relationship is important, yet difficult to measure. SLO's encourage teacher input to the measurement of student growth, but it is still difficult to measure teacher influence, discussed here as a relationship, in an objective manner. From this stems the concern that this vital relationship may not be taken into account in teacher evaluation (Marzano, 2012).

Importance of Value-Added Data

How necessary is the addition of value-added data to the final rating of a practicing teacher? According to a study done by Hanushek & Rivikin, teacher quality is an essential element of student success and school improvement. Their work demonstrates that a student who has a math teacher in the 25th percentile of a quality distribution as opposed to the 75th percentile would lead to a learning increase of 0.2 standard deviations in a school year. (Hanushek & Rivikin, 2010). Therefore, it is critical that teacher impact be represented in the final rating as part of the evaluation.

There are outliers affecting these results, such as validity of tests and measurement error (Hanushek & Rivikin, 2010). However, it is worth noting that based upon study results, replacing 6-10% of a school's weakest teachers with average performing teachers could greatly influence student learning (Hanushek & Rivikin, 2010).

CHAPTER 7

FEEDBACK

Most of us can think of a time when feedback was useful to us. It may not have been formal feedback, but rather a simple, informal suggestion. Anyone who has participated in athletics has likely received feedback from a coach at some time. Comments written by a teacher on a term paper or project may also be considered feedback to the student aspiring to improve a grade or standing in a class.

Why, then, is it so difficult to provide meaningful, consistent feedback concerning job performance? To answer this question, this chapter will define effective feedback and discuss some of the issues surrounding a feedback rich culture in schools.

When training new administrators, I often ask the group how long it takes them to do a typical teacher evaluation. The answers vary, based upon what is required by individual school districts as part of their evaluation plan. But it has usually been determined that an evaluator spends 45-50 minutes observing a classroom, as this is consistent with a middle or high school class period, or a block of subject time in an elementary classroom.

The next phase of the observation progression comes when the evaluator exits the classroom. This is when the evaluator must clean up any scripting or notetaking they have recorded during the observation. Next is the mapping to standards, checking artifacts, lesson plans, and documentation of teacher leadership, as well as conducting pre and post conferences. If you take these hours involved in a single long evaluation, multiply it by each staff member…

This is typically where I see administrators new to the profession begin to panic. In an occupation that is already labor intensive and time starved, they are now being told that the tasks involved in evaluating and providing meaningful feedback will demand that they create even more hours in their day.

Feedback is defined as information that describes performance (Bartz, Thompson, & Rice, 2017). In a lecture at the NeuroLeadership Summit in Boston, Kevin Ochsner of Columbia University stated that people only apply the feedback they receive about 30% of the time (Ochsner, 2010). To have spent 45-60 hours on documentation, preparation, and professional conversation that may have only had a 30% return on employee improvement is concerning to those who analyze effective human resource strategies (Standard for Success Survey Data, 2016). Therefore, as teacher evaluators, we need to maximize the effectiveness of evaluation comments.

Effective feedback is consistent, both in terms of frequency, and free of conflicting messages. It's an ongoing conversation; not a formal event that just takes place every few months. Forbes recently published an online article stating that employees desire consistent feedback; thus, an annual review in isolation is no longer adequate (Bersin, 2013).

To maximize feedback, one must first recognize the value of giving and receiving feedback. In a profession that values a *kids first* philosophy, the first priority of any educator should be building and maintaining positive relationships with students. Next, the daily management and tasks of operations for building administrators is often overwhelming. How can we build and nurture positive relationships with our staff, students, parents, and stakeholders, and still check off all of the items on our to-do lists? Add to this the detailed undertaking of observing staff and providing them with meaningful feedback, and it is no wonder that even experienced administrators may move feedback to the bottom of their priorities.

Employee feedback is fundamental to individual professional growth and improved school culture, which enhances the tasks listed in the previous paragraph. In addition, best practice dictates taking time to identify areas of needed growth for teachers and including student growth as part of the feedback process, and not just checking off boxes on a teacher evaluation form.

The first goal should be creating a feedback rich culture in your school or organization. Feedback should not be a quick comment (remember the post-it note from Chapter One), but rather a part of a larger system. Student assessment should be utilized to measure the effectiveness of teaching practices (Heritage, 2007, as cited in Hollingworth, 2012, p. 366), and frequency and consistency of evaluation practices are also considered in building a strong system of employee evaluation (Darling-Hammond, et al., 2012).

Making Feedback a Priority

Making employee evaluation and feedback a priority is definitely easier said than done. Below are a few points that can help administrators in staying on top of goals for effective teacher evaluation:

1. **Choose the right evaluation tool**. Collecting and managing evaluation data is a huge task. The right employee evaluation tool is key to recording, storing, and analyzing data.

2. **Evaluation process training**. Individual states have their own requirements for training of teacher evaluators. Even if your state does not require training, it is considered best practice. Reach out to neighboring districts, service centers, or professional vendors to gain information on evaluation process training for administrators. Be sure training includes scripting, mapping, and giving teacher feedback. Many districts are also beginning to train their teachers on their evaluation process, to ensure full transparency between evaluators and staff.

3. **Management training.** This differs from number 2, as this is training on the individual system your district chooses for evaluation management. Be sure that all evaluators and teachers have had adequate training to feel comfortable with the system you are using. It is our nature to avoid that which is difficult or that we do not fully understand. Ease of use and comfort with the chosen evaluation system is indispensable.

4. **Schedule time**. Some of these are supposed to be unannounced visits to classrooms, but block it on your personal schedule anyway.

5. **Share the value and importance**. Create a school wide culture of the importance of teacher observation and feedback. Encourage office staff to hold your scheduled evaluation time in reverence and ask unannounced visitors to schedule an appointment for another time. Likewise, ask teachers to have a plan B for minor discipline issues when you are evaluating.

6. **Value the timeframe yourself**. It is tempting, especially when returning from an absence or preparing for an upcoming meeting or event, to skip your intended walkthrough or evaluation time. Barring an absolute emergency, try to stick to the schedule you have created for yourself.

7. **Additional evaluators**. While these management tactics can be useful, nothing replaces help in completion of a task. Also, external evaluators increase inter-rater reliability and thus decrease bias in the evaluation process. Additional evaluators may be department chairs or lead teachers within the district, or may be contracted from professional vendors.

Giving Meaningful Feedback

Once you have built and established a culture in your district or organization that values feedback, it is important to make feedback meaningful and constructive. Too often, we think of feedback as simply a *good job* or *great lesson* comment given in passing. Not to say that this cannot add value to the building of relationships with your staff, but we are finding that today's workforce requires more.

Teachers entering the classroom today are part of the millennial generation, which is designated as those born between 1981 and 1999 (Bartz et al., 2017). Also known as Generation Y, this group seeks input differently and more often than workers of prior generations. According to research, millennials desire coaches rather than bosses (Gallup, Inc., 2016). They prefer those who can mentor and develop their strengths. They are not interested in improvement of areas of weakness, but rather how to foster strengths. Gallup found that while weaknesses do not evolve into strengths, strengths mature continually.

This may seem in contrast with our previous discussion on feedback and targeting weaknesses as areas for improvement. However, it is consistent with the Gallup research that organizations should, "minimize weaknesses and maximize strengths" (Gallup, Inc., 2016, p. 3). In order to maximize a teacher's strengths, we must identify them through teacher evaluation and observation.

For example, I know of several principals who departmentalize their staffs based upon teaching strengths. The simplest example of this is the principal who has two fifth grade teachers, one of whom is strong at teaching math and the other who is stronger at teaching language arts. It makes sense to have these teachers teach their subject of strength twice, and have the students switch classes to receive the benefits of the enhanced instruction.

When we use a system of teacher evaluation, based upon an instructional framework rubric, we can expand this example to a much broader context, as it lets us identify strengths and weaknesses in specific domains to provide targeted feedback, thus creating a culture of communication and direction for strength development. Gallup does not suggest that we do not address weaknesses, but that we focus on strength development when creating our workplace culture (Gallup, Inc. 2016).

Most of us prefer feedback to be immediate, and this is definitely true for millennials. Gallup tells us that millennials don't want an annual review, but instead prefer a continual process of communication (Gallup, Inc. 2016). This may be due in part to their use of and access to social media, as they are now used to receiving immediate responses in real time.

The conflict comes into play when a millennial is being evaluated or reviewed by someone of another generation. If a supervisor or evaluator is from an older generation, they may not recognize this need of millennials for continual feedback. Further, a millennial may be viewed by someone from an older generation as a "job hopper" (Gallup, Inc., 2016 p. 7) when the reality may be that they are changing jobs due to lack of engagement in their current role. Increased interaction and feedback from supervisors leads to increased engagement of employees (Gallup, Inc., 2016). In reference to the education world, where beginning teachers are coming to us from the millennial generation, and we see more of them leaving the profession or changing schools at an alarming rate, we need to question if this could be due to lack of engagement and meaningful feedback.

Maximizing all Feedback

There is often a perception that to be constructive, feedback must always be positive. This is notably true in the education world, where a high value is placed upon positive reinforcement to build and nurture relationships with students.

Robert Pozen, a senior lecturer at Harvard Business School, writes that "people generally respond more strongly to negative events than positive ones." (Pozen, 2013, para. 2). He cites a workplace study that found employees react six times more strongly to negative interactions with their boss, and nearly half of employees on the receiving end of harsh criticism intentionally reduce their productivity (Miner, as cited by Pozen, 2013).

At the same time, 57 percent of employees surveyed by Zenger/ Folkman, a leadership consultancy firm, prefer corrective feedback over praise, and 92 percent agreed with the statement, "Negative (redirecting) feedback, *if delivered appropriately*, is effective at improving performance" (Zenger & Folkman, 2014, para. 8). Note the emphasis on *if delivered appropriately*.

Some common pitfalls for giving feedback are as follows:

- Not giving feedback at all
- Letting it pile up
- Not setting clear expectations
- Giving vague feedback
- Doing all of the talking
- Prescribing solutions

(Cydcor, 2018).

By contrast, below are some tips for providing meaningful feedback:

- Create safety

- Be positive
- Be specific
- Be immediate
- Be tough, not mean

(Halford 2011).

Effective feedback is consistent, both in terms of frequency, and free of conflicting messages. It's an ongoing conversation; not a formal event that just takes place every few months. Building a continuous feedback system is really the best way to contribute to growth and provide employees with the direction they need. Changing the format of your teacher evaluations to a more fluid, ongoing method will make all the difference in the world.

Imagine being a beginning teacher struggling with classroom management. Does that teacher need help in August, December, or April? This is somewhat of a trick question, because while the first *right* answer may appear to be August, the actual answer is *all of the above*! Our teachers and students benefit from consistent, constructive, timely feedback. Think about the veteran teacher who is likely doing a fantastic job and doesn't need feedback. Or do they? If we think of feedback as only criticism, we are inclined to skip those who are doing a great job. In reality, we all need feedback (positive and negative). Take the time to reinforce what these employees are doing well, and they will continue doing so.

CHAPTER 8

INTER-RATER RELIABILITY

A description of a strong teacher evaluation system is not complete without discussion on inter-rater reliability. Inter-rater reliability is vital to employee evaluation practice to eliminate biases and sustain transparency, consistency, and impartiality (Tillema, as cited in Soslau & Lewis, 2014, p. 21). In addition, a data-driven system of evaluation creating a feedback rich culture is considered best practice.

Examination by school leadership of quantitative trend data and comparison of evaluators is the essence of professional growth (Graham, Milanowski, & Miller, as cited in Soslau & Lewis, 2014, p. 39). Assurance of inter-rater reliability decreases biases and increases ethical practice in the evaluation procedure.

The purpose of ensuring inter-rater reliability is two-fold. First and most obvious, inter-rater reliability is the practice of ensuring that there is more than one set of eyes evaluating a teacher. Requiring multiple observations by various administrative staff increases inter-rater reliability. In a school with multiple administrators, or a principal and assistant principal, this is fairly easy to manage. Some smaller schools just have one administrator per building. This creates an issue for the building administrator not only to complete all evaluations, but to have a second voice when gathering data during observations or making decisions on teacher effectiveness. Multiple observations conducted by these evaluators are crucial to sustained inter-rater reliability as well.

The second element of inter-rater reliability is ensuring that all evaluators are looking for the same traits of good teaching. The pre-determined rubric is certainly helpful with this, but individual interpretation can lead to different understandings of what good instruction *looks like*. This requires on-going conversation and training of administrative teams.

Leadership

It is ultimately the responsibility of school leadership to analyze and track data to ensure that observations are being completed with fidelity. If this is not the case, then additional administrative training may be beneficial. Let's look at a case study of a small rural school that is working to ensure inter-rater reliability:

South Harrison School Corporation is a small rural school in southern Indiana. Their superintendent reached out to staff members of Standard For Success, who have been providing an online system for managing their teacher evaluation process for several years. The goal of the school district was increased inter-rater reliability, and they were in search of facilitators to guide this discussion among their administrative team. Keep in mind that this is a small district and that observations by multiple administrators could have been a challenge. Therefore, the building principals in the district were scheduled to *trade* buildings and act as a secondary evaluator in another building. This solved the problem of multiple evaluators in a building, but the district leadership team wanted to take things a step further. Their focus was the second element of inter-rater reliability, ensuring that all evaluators in the district were identifying what good instruction looks like in their district. For example, while the district rubric contained an indicator on student engagement, what does student engagement look like?

The next task, following conversations and discussion on the traits of good instruction, was which of these to include in their walk-through observation check list. By identifying and discussing these as a team, not only is inter-rater reliability enhanced, but now the

walk-through checklist allows evaluators to gather more data on those areas of instruction most valued by the district. The compilation of this data is then available for the administrative team to analyze in future meetings.

While this was an amazing day of conversation for this particular administrative team, it is important to note that their discussion is ongoing. As observations are completed, it is best practice to periodically meet as a team to analyze the collected data to distinguish areas of strengths and weaknesses among evaluators and define characteristics of specific instructional domains. This continued nurturing of the elements of inter-rater reliability will help eliminate bias and keep the focus on professional growth.

Assigning a numerical value to teacher effectiveness based upon a pre-determined rubric helps to decrease bias. The rubric is certainly a guiding force in this practice, but there still needs to be local conversation. As stated in the previous example, most teacher evaluation rubrics include an indicator on student engagement, along with examples of what an evaluator might see students doing to demonstrate this. However, it is still crucial to discuss local norms. Does this mean that all students are sitting in their seat, with eyes on the speaker? Does it mean that students are involved in a hands-on activity? Maybe it is a combination of both of these, or student behaviors that reflect a local initiative.

As administrative teams participate in these tasks, it is critical that all parties view this as a growth exercise. As with any part of the observation and evaluation process, we are not looking to find one correct answer to the question. Rather, we are encouraging conversation among our leadership teams about what we value and look for during observations of instructional practices. Since the *look* of good instruction remains a matter of local control, these frequent conversations, along with norming activities, help evaluators become more consistent in their evaluation practices.

Analysis of Data

These conversational meetings are also a good time for leadership teams to begin analyzing their data, as it relates to inter-rater reliability. We know that strengths and challenges of teachers can be identified with the evaluation data, but in reference to inter-rater reliability, we are looking at trends among various evaluators. If a specific evaluator has a high number of highly effective marks in their building, this can become a talking point for the team. Is this evaluator looking for the same traits and holding teachers to the same standard as the other evaluators in the district? Or is their staff exceptional in this area of instruction? Again, the purpose is not to call an evaluator out or tell them that they are *doing it wrong*. But both of these pieces of information are valuable to district leadership. If the evaluator is inflating observation scores, more in-depth conversation and training may be required to help this individual grow professionally as an evaluator. If the staff in this building is exemplary, opportunities may exist for this evaluator and their teachers to become leaders in the district for the areas of instruction in which they excel. Likewise, a large number of ineffective ratings in a specific domain signals a need for this building leader to increase professional development in this instructional domain for their staff.

Norming Activities

Norming activities that permit evaluators to *co-evaluate* either teaching videos or actual classroom visits and then compare results help evaluators become more consistent in their practices. These can be done via teaching videos during an administrative meeting, or actual classroom visits by the team. Often teams have building principals and evaluators watch a commercial video of a teacher interacting with students and script what they see. This is excellent practice in scripting, but also serves as a conversation starter on *what did we see?*. This can lead to the next essential question, which is *what are we looking for?*. Once the team is proficient at scripting, they can take it to the next level and discuss where that piece of evidence would land when mapping to the rubric. These continual conversations increase understanding of a district's expectations and thus inter-rater reliability.

As educational leaders, we have a responsibility to ensure that evaluation practices are fair and consistent in order to establish trust among those being evaluated. When evaluation data is discussed with the teacher in a transparent manner, we once again help build the culture of growth and improvement. This can not only help teachers enrich their craft, but can be a game changer in terms of improving instruction for students.

CHAPTER 9

TEACHER DISMISSAL

In Chapter Two, we discussed why we evaluate. This chapter is intended to dig deeper into this question, including practical reasons for the school administrator to evaluate teachers and provide meaningful feedback to their subordinates, leading to benefits for the school district as a whole.

My hope is that this book, and this chapter in particular, reflect the tone of my personal philosophy that evaluation and feedback not be used for punitive purposes. Rather, that these are utilized as growth exercises that help those around us develop professionally. If that is the case, then I hope this question will evoke an easy answer:

Is the purpose of teacher evaluation teacher improvement, or teacher dismissal?

By choosing teacher improvement (as I hope all readers do!), we are not discounting or ignoring that sometimes teacher dismissal is necessary. There are times when we must use our evaluation data to lead courageous conversations with those for whom teaching is not their forte. However, it is the hope of this writer that these instances occur only in severe circumstances (a teacher poses a threat to a student) or after significant attempts to guide this teacher to improve are not successful. There are also cases where retaining a teacher is actually doing a disservice to our students. Overall, we know that the evaluation process must not be one of targeting individuals for dismissal, but rather one of constructive feedback and identification of areas for individual improvement.

Dismissal of an Ineffective Teacher

Dismissing an ineffective teacher, or any employee, may be one of the most difficult tasks that an administrator will face in their career. Even when procedures are established and followed appropriately, there will likely be some form of appeal from the individual, and the emotional side of teacher dismissal will still come in to play. Administrators recognize that employee termination places a burden on an individual's career and ability to provide for one's family. That being said, dismissal of ineffective teachers is often necessary for improvement of the school and to provide students with the best educational opportunities possible.

Definition of an Ineffective Teacher

The first step in dismissing an ineffective teacher is establishing a definition of an ineffective teacher. This has received much attention in recent years. As a result of legislation on teacher evaluation, most local education agencies are allowed to define an ineffective teacher as a part of their teacher evaluation system. Evaluators now have a rubric or list of traits to observe in order to designate a teacher's effectiveness. Multiple measures stipulations require schools to incorporate some measure of student growth data into the effectiveness rating, as we discussed in Chapter Five.

Concerns

While a firm evaluation policy may make teacher evaluation and ultimately teacher dismissal less subjective, there are concerns. In a 2012 article, Robert Marzano refers to the RATE (Rapid Assessment of Teacher Effectiveness) as an instrument designed to determine teacher effectiveness. However, Marzano notes that missing from the RATE list are elements such as the teacher-student relationship and classroom management, which are recognized in studies on effective teaching (Marzano, 2012).

Another concern comes from Skourdoumbis, who states that labeling teacher effectiveness "positions classroom teachers as the controlling influence and primary participants in determining the academic achievement of their students". He further comments that contemporary education policy has focused on utilizing more effective teaching strategies to improve student achievement (Skourdoumbis, 2013).

Documentation

Key to teacher dismissal is that of documentation. Regardless of the school district or organization's policies that have been established for employee termination, all correspondence and steps will require thorough documentation. It is also outlined in many states' evaluation legislation that evaluation be tied to data and stored in a system to be available for review by all parties to increase transparency.

When analyzing the dismissal of ineffective teachers, there is an ethical side to consider. As asked previously, is the goal of the administration dismissal, or improvement of the individual? Certainly, in the beginning stages, one can assume that when considering the high cost of employee turnover, improvement of performance would be preferable. As stated in Chapter Two, Palestini writes "A subordinate depends on his or her superiors for assistance in accomplishing a task and identifying obstacles to achieving a work goal." (Palestini, 2011). Therefore, we can assume that evaluations are not best utilized for targeting individuals for dismissal, but rather to provide constructive criticism and feedback for individual improvement.

Appeals Procedure

As ineffective teachers are dismissed, it stands to reason that there are going to be those who fight the dismissal, perhaps all the way into the court system. At this time, it appears that both state and federal courts are declining ruling on teacher evaluation systems. Since the role of the courts has been to determine if local laws and established policies have been followed and if teachers were given due process, teachers have been unsuccessful in obtaining a ruling on what they feel is an unfair or inadequate evaluation system (Popham, W. J., & DeSander, M., 2014). While this is news that may make teachers undergoing dismissal uncomfortable, it is supportive of administrators implementing dismissal. As long as a set of local policies is pre-determined, implemented, and documented, dismissal of ineffective teachers should stand. Of greater importance, as we continue to build a culture of feedback and communication, teachers and administrators begin to feel more collaborative in the evaluation process and recognize that all parties are acting in the best interest of students.

The chart on the following page represents some commonly used steps in the teacher dismissal process. While it is not intended to be an absolute, it may provide guidance that can be adapted to epitomize a school districts' local norms. In Chapter Ten, we look further into teacher attrition and why it is in everyone's best interest to develop and retain our current teachers, so that dismissal is not as often necessary.

TEACHER DISMISSAL

Definitions:

Probationary teacher—usually a beginning teacher with less than two years of teaching experience.

Professional teacher—usually a veteran teacher with more than two years of teaching experience.

Negative impact—a significant decrease in student achievement and notably low levels of student growth.

Sufficient progress—meets all remediation goals.

Insufficient progress—does not meet all remediation goals.

Growth plan—improvement plan of specific goals developed by the teacher and evaluator.

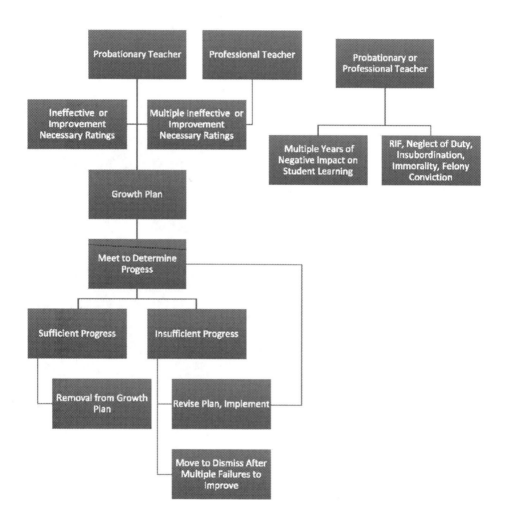

CHAPTER 10

TEACHER GROWTH, DEVELOPMENT, AND ATTRITION

In the not so distant past, graduates of teacher education programs were scrambling for employment, sometimes only to be laid off a few years later. These Reduction in Force (RIF) procedures were so common during the 1990's and early 2000's that most beginning teachers felt fortunate to have a teaching position and seldom left it to explore other options.

Fast forward 20-25 years, and young beginning teachers of the millennial generation are shopping schools to find the teaching situation that best fits their needs and preferences. If they are unhappy where they are, another school is hiring next year.

Within the next ten years, this shortage is expected to continue, with an alarming loss of 100,000 teachers annually (Darling-Hammond, as cited by Stratford, 2016). This group cites concern over low enrollment in teacher education programs and increasing student enrollment in prek-12 schools.

The teacher attrition rate, or percentage of teachers who either change schools or exit the profession, is 16% for the public-school sector alone (Redding, 2018). Of those leaving the teaching profession annually, less than one-third are retiring (Carver-Thomas & Darling-Hammond, 2017). Teachers seem to be exiting teaching positions in high poverty schools twice as quickly as those in more affluent areas.

There are several theories as to why this attrition rate is on the rise. Many cite low pay, the demands of excessive student testing, and increased violent behaviors on the part of students as possible causes. Some are even comparing the number of teachers who attended traditional teacher preparation programs to those who transitioned to education from other programs, and found that there may be more teachers leaving who come from non-traditional pathways into the profession (Redding, 2018).

A lack of supportive environment has also been cited as a factor in teacher turnover. While this may appear to be obvious, a study in subsequent chapters will discuss this in greater detail. A 2016 study by Standard For Success found that teachers who receive frequent, consistent feedback are less likely to become frustrated and leave the profession (Standard For Success Survey Data, 2016). Since this is the case, we must, as school leaders, find ways to encourage and support our existing teachers. Not only is it the ethical thing to do, but it is the most cost effective as well. New research suggests that it costs more than $20,000 to replace a teacher in an urban setting (Barnes, G., Crowe, E., & Schaefer, B., as cited by Carver-Thomas, & Darling Hammond, 2017). This does not include salary replacement, only the cost of teacher search, recruitment, and training. Considering the high cost of employee turnover, improvement of performance is preferable to teacher dismissal. Of greater cost is the loss of instructional time for students during a transition of teachers in a classroom.

Teacher Retention and Attrition

As our nation faces this teacher shortage and increasing teacher attrition rate, it is more important than ever to retain and develop those currently practicing in the classroom. This once again highlights the importance of meaningful feedback in this growth and development process. Further findings report that the treatment of an evaluation system that provides analysis of performance indicators and cultivates a feedback rich culture has a positive impact on professional growth and development of teachers as measured by evaluation data, as these teachers not only showed improvement in instructional indicators, but were less likely to leave their school or profession. This reinforces the need for administrators to realize the value of analyzing their own district data for the purpose of helping to grow and retain teachers.

As administrators, what can we do to decrease teacher attrition and improve teacher recruitment and retention? Most of us have limited control over salary increases, as schools are faced with diminishing budgets. But as stated above, the issues often run deeper than a heftier paycheck. As with so many elements of teacher evaluation, there is not one cure-all for decreasing teacher turnover. However, research has cited a few general examples of how to attract and retain teachers:

1. **Dedicate resources toward employee feedback.** We discussed in detail the importance of targeted, continuous feedback in Chapter Five. According to a Gallup survey, companies that provide regular employee evaluation or feedback have a 15% lower turnover rate than companies that do not (Gallup, 2013).

2. **Show sincere interest in teachers' development.** As a teacher, I often dreaded professional development days, as they were not meaningful for my own self-improvement. That is not an arrogant statement to imply that I could not benefit from the topic of training, but simply that I usually did not have ownership in the topic as it related to my own personal goals and development. We must be strategic in providing dedicated resources that address specific areas at different levels.

3. **Seek methods to be more progressive.** Give teachers the tools needed to be more effective in the classroom. Seek ways to help teachers integrate technology and other progressive platforms that engage students. Often, foundations and local businesses allocate funding for these initiatives.

4. **Encourage teacher input.** Whether we are talking about teacher evaluation, overall school goals, or innovations, give teachers a voice on key initiatives. The more that they are involved in setting the course for the school's direction, the more likely they feel invested in future outcomes. Teachers who feel empowered are less likely to feel disengaged.

PART II

CHAPTER 11

PURPOSE OF STUDY

In 2016, I was asked to lead a research team on teacher evaluation in the state of Indiana. The evaluation management software (platform) for which I worked knew from client feedback that their product was making the jobs of administrators, lead teachers, and other evaluators easier and providing them with viable data. However, their desire was to examine the impact on teachers. Were those using the product showing improvement in performance, and were they more likely to stay in the profession?

Our team began by mapping common indicators across various rubrics. For example, a school evaluating a standard on a rubric stating *3/4 of students are engaged* and another evaluating that *more than half of the students are engaged* are evaluating the same expectation, just utilizing different language. Therefore, a commonality exists in the standard being evaluated, and our team wanted these to be matched in our data analysis.

Initially, a computer program was utilized to detect common terminology among indicators. The team then conducted a document analysis to determine if the indicators were representative of the skill being assessed in the common rubric indicator. Those indicators that did not align to the common rubric were eliminated from the study.

This study was designed to analyze data in the instructional domain of teachers who had been evaluated utilizing the Standard for Success teacher evaluation software. The research questions were: 1) What was the impact of Standard for Success as a system of teacher evaluation management and feedback? 2) Was there improvement in teacher performance as represented by evaluation data of those teachers whose schools had utilized Standard for Success consistently over a three-year period? Quantitative data was collected in the Standard for Success system over a three-year period. A comparative study was conducted utilizing 2016 SFS data between a cohort and non-cohort group of teachers. Teachers in the cohort group had utilized Standard for Success for three consecutive years, those in the non-cohort group had utilized Standard for Success for less than three years. The experimental two-group design was created to determine if a significant difference existed between the cohort and non-cohort groups. An analysis of trend data over a three-year period of the cohort group was analyzed as well. Analysis of collected data showed that there was a significant difference between the cohort and non-cohort groups. In addition, the cohort group demonstrated significant improvement measured by trend data over a three-year period. Based on findings, it was concluded that the treatment of an evaluation system that provided analysis of performance indicators and cultivated a feedback rich culture had a positive impact on professional growth and development of teachers as measured by evaluation data.

As explained in previous chapters, many school districts have local control in choosing their evaluation rubric. Therefore, we chose the most commonly utilized rubric among the schools utilizing our platform to serve as a consistent teacher evaluation rubric. Other rubrics were aligned with fidelity by instructional indicators. Both the cohort and non-cohort groups of teachers may have been at any phase in their practicing career. The cohort group had been evaluated utilizing our platform for three years; this group had a minimum of three years of teaching experience.

It is important to point out a few delimitations and assumptions of our study. We limited our research group to those schools in our state utilizing our Standard for Success platform that voluntarily gave permission for their non-identifying teacher evaluation data to be used for this study. While use of the platform was the treatment analyzed between the cohort and non-cohort groups, there may have existed differences among opportunities for professional development, training of evaluators, and administrative turnover.

An assumption of the study was that our common platform was a valid measure of teacher evaluation and that other evaluation rubrics were aligned with fidelity. It was also assumed that the teachers in this study were a representative population of teachers and that evaluators were appropriately trained in the evaluation process.

Our first hypothesis was that there would be a significant difference in ratings of instructional domains during observations of teachers in the cohort group over a three-year period. The second hypothesis was that there would be a significant difference in ratings of instructional domains during observations of teachers in the cohort group and the non-cohort group. In other words, did the teachers utilizing the platform improve over a three-year period, and were those who had been utilizing the platform over a three-year period receive higher rankings than those utilizing the platform for less than three years?

Trend Data

Number of teachers for each rating (highly effective, effective, improvement necessary, ineffective) for 2013-14 and 2015-16 were entered on an Excel 2011 spreadsheet in preparation for the hypothesis test. A one-tailed paired *t*-test was conducted to determine if a significant difference existed between the ratings from 2013-14 and 2015-16. Tables and graphs on the following pages display the results. A coefficient of df=17 was significant at the level p=0.05, the critical value of *t* being 2.11. There was a significant difference between the beginning and ending ratings in three categories (highly effective, improvement necessary, and ineffective). There was no significant difference found in the effective category. Therefore, the null hypothesis, which stated that there would be no significant difference in ratings of instructional domains during observations of teachers utilizing Standard for Success for three years, was rejected for three categories (highly effective, improvement necessary, and ineffective). The null was retained for the effective category, as there was no significant difference found between beginning and ending ratings over the three-year period in this category. All data were analyzed at the 0.05 level of significance, yielding a 95% confidence level that the findings would be due to the impact of Standard for Success.

DIANNA WHITLOCK, ED.D.

Cohort vs. Non-Cohort Groups

Percentages of teachers for each rating (highly effective, effective, improvement necessary, ineffective) for the cohort and non-cohort groups were entered on an Excel 2011 spreadsheet in preparation for the hypothesis test. A one-tailed independent *t*-test was conducted to determine if a significant difference existed between the two groups. Tables and graphs on following pages display the results. A coefficient of *df*=17 was significant at the level p=0.05, the critical value of *t* being 2.11. There was a significant difference between the cohort and non-cohort groups in all rating categories (highly effective, effective, improvement necessary, and ineffective). Therefore, the null hypothesis, which stated that there would be no significant difference in ratings of instructional domains during observations of teachers in the cohort group and those in the non-cohort group, was rejected. All data were analyzed at the 0.05 level of significance, yielding a 95% confidence level that the findings would be due to the impact of Standard for Success.

CHAPTER 12

STUDY FINDINGS

This section examines the results of the trend data analysis and the comparative study. Data from the teacher evaluation system were compiled and analyzed to determine the first hypothesis, which was that there would be a significant difference in scores of teachers in the cohort group over a three-year period. The second hypothesis tested was that there would be a significant difference in ratings of instructional domains during observations of teachers in the cohort group and those in the non-cohort group (Whitlock, 2016).

Data housed in the Standard for Success teacher evaluation system was utilized for analysis. Non-identifying teacher evaluation data from participating schools was extracted and analyzed following rubric alignment. For the first analysis, trend evaluation data of the cohort group of teachers were tracked from 2013-2016. The second analysis compared 2016 evaluation data between a cohort group of teachers who had utilized SFS for three years to a non-cohort group who had used SFS for less than three years. The treatment for this analysis was the use of Standard for Success.

In order to provide a commonality for comparison, the SFS research team utilized a common framework for rubric alignment. Therefore, all indicators utilized in this study were deemed equivalent in the instructional domain. Initially, a computer program was utilized to detect common terminology among indicators. The team then conducted a document analysis to determine if the indicators were representative of the skill being assessed in the rubric indicator. Those indicators that did not align to rubric indicators were eliminated from the study. Data was assessed by rating (highly effective, effective, improvement necessary, and ineffective) in order to compare the number of teachers rated in each of these categories.

Trend Data of Cohort Group

Highly Effective

	2013-14	2015-16
Number of teachers	4162	4162
Ratings	19,725	21,865
Mean	52.6588889	58.3722222
Median	53.58	57.54
Mode	NA	NA
Standard Deviation	16.98928519	15.56269319

The table above displays the results of teachers rated as highly effective in the cohort groups from 2013-14 to 2015-16. Ratings represent the number of highly effective scores for instructional domain indicators. There was a higher mean score of teachers rated as highly effective in the instructional indicators in the 2015-16 school year than in the 2013-14 school year.

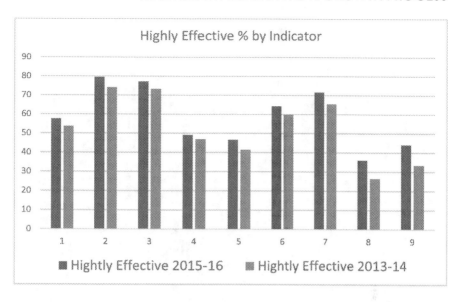

Effective

	2013-14	2015-16
Number of teachers	4162	4162
Ratings	31,103	31,455
Mean	83.03333333	83.97333333
Median	83.71	82.77
Mode	NA	NA
Standard Deviation	9.23170488	6.129459601

The table above displays the results of teachers rated as effective in the cohort groups from 2013-14 and 2015-16. Ratings represent the number of highly effective scores for instructional domain indicators. There was a slightly higher mean score of teachers rated as effective in the instructional indicators in the 2015-16 school year than in the 2013-14 school year.

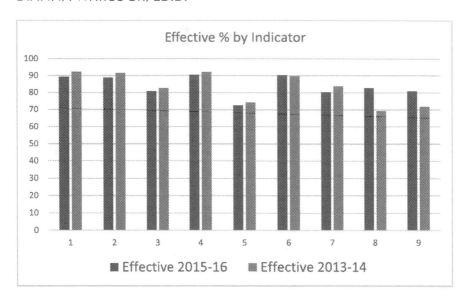

Improvement Necessary

	2013-14	2015-16
Number of teachers	4162	4162
Ratings	2,689	1,399
Mean	7.177777778	3.736666667
Median	6.94	3.87
Mode	NA	NA
Standard Deviation	3.663208217	1.684094712

The table above displays the results of teachers rated as improvement necessary in the cohort groups from 2013-14 and 2015-16. Ratings represent the number of improvement necessary scores for instructional domain indicators. There was a lower mean score of teachers rated as improvement necessary in the instructional indicators in the 2015-16 school year than in the 2013-14 school year.

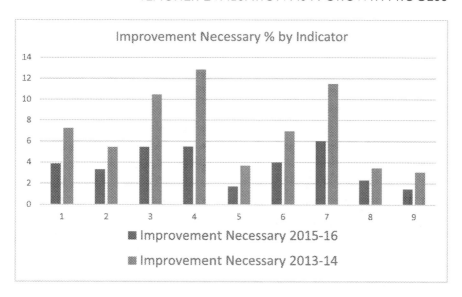

Ineffective

	2013-14	2015-16
Number of teachers	4162	4162
Ratings	350	156
Mean	0.934444444	0.416666667
Median	0.62	0.34
Mode	NA	0.34
Standard Deviation	0.839153012	0.343693177

The table above displays the results of teachers rated as ineffective in the cohort groups from 2013-14 and 2015-16. Ratings represent the number of ineffective scores for instructional domain indicators. There was a lower mean score of teachers rated as ineffective in the instructional indicators in the 2015-16 school year than in the 2013-14 school year.

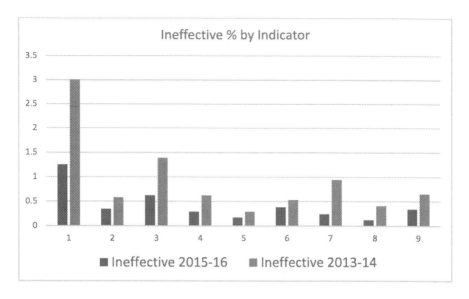

Cohort vs. Non-Cohort Groups

Highly Effective

	Cohort	Non-Cohort
Number of teachers	4162	8001
Ratings	21,865	19,359
Mean	58.3722	35.9411
Median	57.54	34.12
Mode	NA	NA
Standard Deviation	15.5626932	10.8610272

The table above displays the results of teachers rated as highly effective in the cohort and non-cohort groups. Ratings represent the number of highly effective scores for instructional domain indicators. There was a higher mean score of teachers rated as highly effective in the instructional indicators within the cohort group than the non-cohort group.

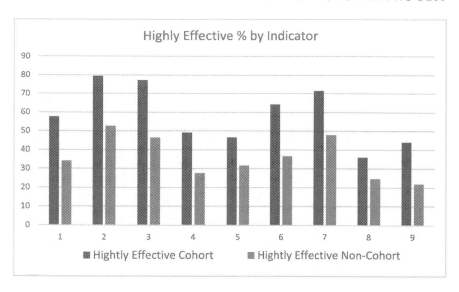

Effective

	Cohort	Non-Cohort
Number of teachers	4162	8001
Ratings	31,455	41,764
Mean	83.9733	77.5344
Median	82.77	79.1
Mode	N/A	N/A
Standard Deviation	6.1294596	6.04899395

The table above displays the results of teachers rated as effective in the cohort and non-cohort groups. Ratings represent the number of effective scores for instructional domain indicators. There was a higher mean score of teachers rated as effective in the instructional indicators within the cohort group than the non-cohort group.

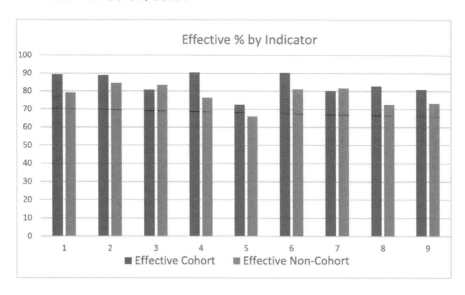

Improvement Necessary

	Cohort	Non-Cohort
Number of teachers	4162	8001
Ratings	1,399	5,907
Mean	3.7367	10.9667
Median	3.87	11.36
Mode	N/A	N/A
Standard Deviation	1.68409471	3.89703092

The table above displays the results of teachers rated as improvement necessary in the cohort and non-cohort groups. Ratings represent the number of improvement necessary scores for instructional domain indicators. There was a lower mean score of teachers rated as improvement necessary in the instructional indicators within the cohort group than the non-cohort group.

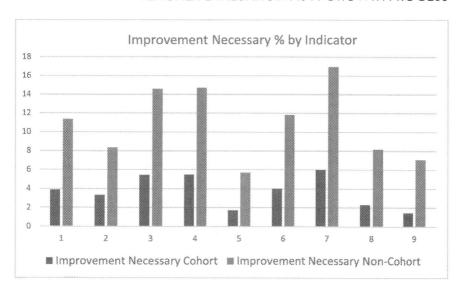

Ineffective

	Cohort	Non-Cohort
Number of teachers	4162	8001
Ratings	156	1,041
Mean	0.4167	1.9322
Median	0.34	1.62
Mode	0.34	N/A
Standard Deviation	0.34369318	0.88502511

The table above displays the results of teachers rated as ineffective in the cohort and non-cohort groups. Ratings represent the number of ineffective scores for instructional domain indicators. There was a lower mean score of teachers rated as ineffective in the instructional indicators within the cohort group than the non-cohort group.

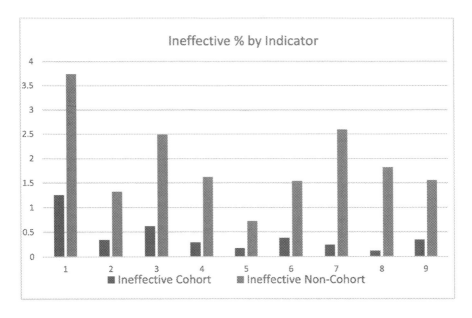

Evaluation of Findings and Results

Table 1
Trend Data of Cohort Group

	Probability t	Critical t	df	Significance	Retain/Reject
Highly eff.	0.000119287	2.11	17	0.05	reject
Effective	0.327498146				retain
Imp. Nec.	0.000560115				reject
Ineffective	0.008277207				reject

As a result of a significant difference that existed in the highly effective, improvement necessary, and ineffective ratings, the null hypothesis that there would be no significant difference in ratings of the instructional domain during observations of teachers in the cohort group over a three-year period was rejected. The null was retained for the effective category, as there was no significant difference in ratings of this category during observations of teachers in the cohort group over a three-year period.

Table 2
Cohort vs. Non-Cohort Group

	Probability t	Critical t	df	Significance	Retain/Reject
Highly eff.	0.00156683	2.11	17	0.05	reject
Effective	0.01970228				reject
Imp. Nec.	0.00017518				reject
Ineffective	0.00033322				reject

As a result of a significant difference that existed in all rating categories, the null hypothesis that there would be no significant difference in ratings of instructional indicators during observations of teachers in the cohort group and those in the non-cohort group was rejected.

Summary of Findings

This study analyzed the relationship between teacher effectiveness ratings and use of a teacher evaluation system. Specifically, the research questions were 1) Was there improvement in teacher performance as represented by evaluation data of those teachers whose schools have utilized Standard for Success consistently over a three-year period? and 2) What was the impact of Standard for Success as a system of teacher evaluation management and feedback?

In the analysis of trend data, a significant difference existed among the highly effective, improvement necessary, and ineffective category ratings. There was no significant difference in the effective category rating from the 2013-14 school year to the 2015-16 school year.

In the comparative study between the cohort and non-cohort groups, a significant difference was found in all rating categories for the instructional indicators during observations of teachers.

Less Than Proficient Markings

Teacher evaluation data from both groups (cohort and non-cohort) of teachers was collected in the Standard for Success evaluation software. While specific percentages by sub indicator were excluded from the statistical portion of this study, researchers examined percentages of the representative sample of Indiana teachers who were marked less than proficient in instructional indicators under the instructional domain. This data was analyzed for support of the statistical findings in this study, and could be utilized to drive professional development and programming for teacher education preparation.

The area with the largest number of teachers marked less than proficient was 2.7, maximizing instructional time, with 14.09% of teachers in this sample marked less than proficient. This was a slight increase from 2013, when 13.75% of teachers were marked less than proficient in this indicator. Since the cohort group showed statistical improvement in this indicator, the decrease in overall proficiency may have been within the non-cohort group, as this group scored significantly higher in the improvement necessary and ineffective areas than the cohort group for this indicator.

The second highest percentage was found in indicator 2.3, student engagement, with 12.75% of teachers scoring less than proficient. However, this 2016 percentage was actually a decrease from 2013 (13.46%). The next two areas of concern for practicing teachers were 2.1 (student understanding and mastery of lesson objective) and 2.4 (checks for understanding). Indicator 2.1 had 11% of teachers practicing below the level of proficiency, and 2.4 demonstrated 11.9%.

Implications of Findings

Trend Data

When analyzing the movement of the cohort group from the 2013-14 school year to the 2015-16 school year, the only category for which the research does not support a significant difference in instructional improvement was the effective category. Although there was a slight practical difference from the first year to the third, no significant statistical difference was found. One possible reason for this was the movement of teachers from one category to another. For example, as teachers grew professionally, some who were in the effective category during the 2013-14 school year may have moved into the highly effective category by 2015-2016. Likewise, some may have scored in the improvement necessary category in the first year and moved to the effective category by year three. Overall, there were more teachers in the highly effective and effective categories in year three than year one, and fewer teachers in the improvement necessary and ineffective categories in year three than year one.

Cohort vs. Non-Cohort

There was a statistically larger number of cohort teachers in the highly effective and effective categories. There were statistically fewer cohort teachers in the improvement necessary and ineffective categories. Since the treatment of this study was the Standard for Success teacher evaluation platform, researchers concluded that teachers who had this system providing a common framework for teacher evaluation saw improved evaluation ratings. This was consistent with the findings of Darling-Hammond, et al., (2012), who supported a feedback rich culture as part of a system containing trained evaluators, professional growth for employees, and procedures for due process.

Application of Findings

The statistical data in this study could be used to drive individualized professional development for teachers. By analyzing the samples' strengths and weaknesses by indicator, professional development could be tailored to accommodate a specific area of instruction. This supportive culture of consistent conversation and meaningful feedback between administrator and teacher could lead to improvement in teacher effectiveness. Ultimately, the goal was that teachers would feel supported and experience success in the classroom, which could result in higher rates of teacher retention. It could be further generalized that improvement in instruction will lead to improvement in student achievement.

The second application of the findings of this study would be to drive programming in higher education. As colleges and universities prepare aspiring teachers, having access to data demonstrating the instructional indicators in which practicing educators are struggling could impact curricular decisions.

CHAPTER 13

FINDINGS IN PRACTICE

Conducting this study gave us the data reported in Chapter Twelve, and an academic analysis of the importance of a system of frequent, consistent feedback. We found that teachers utilizing the platform improved over a three-year period, and that those who had utilized the system for a three-year period received higher marks than those who had used the system for less than three years. Also, the teachers who utilized the system over a three-year period were less transient than those who had not.

But there were some other items that stood out to us as well. For example, the fact that so many teachers were struggling with similar indicators led us to conclude that these indicators may not be stressed enough in teacher education preparation programs or professional development. This brought our research team to pose some deeper questions as to how we, as educational leaders, can continue to improve evaluation for teacher growth, development, and retention.

What if we could report and analyze the actual ratings behind the final markings?

It is key to point out that most states only require that a school district report a final evaluation score for teachers. The teachers in this study had been rated as Highly Effective, Effective, Improvement Necessary, or Ineffective (1,2,3,4). Ultimately, their state department of education only saw the final number. Our study drilled deeper into the markings behind these final ratings, looking at the specific indicators marked for participating teachers. As a result, 98% of the teachers in the study, while struggling with specific indicators, were given a final rating of Effective or Highly Effective, and 10% were not given a final rating at all (Indiana Department of Education, 2017). At the same time, our more in-depth analysis revealed that 14% of these same teachers were marked less than effective in maximizing instructional time. 13% were marked less than effective in student engagement, and 11% were marked less than effective in developing student understanding. This brought us to question the markings behind the final rating, and what they really mean.

With this type of in-depth analysis, we began to question if the final marks are being inflated. This question is not intended to imply that educators are conducting unethical practices, but rather that there may exist a lack of training in conducting and managing the evaluation process. Additionally, administrative teams that are not having frequent conversations on inter-rater reliability and analyzing evaluation data may struggle with assigning finalizations that are reflective of the teachers' performance.

Like so many other tasks of administrators, much of this comes back to time management. We know that administrators are beyond busy and wear multiple hats daily. If an administrator does not have a system of collecting and reporting evaluation data, the tasks associated with teacher evaluation can quickly become overwhelming. Not only may an administrator struggle with making time to analyze the data to assign a final ranking reflective of the teacher's performance, but without a management platform that generates data reports, this may be impossible to break down.

What if we could report strengths and challenges of the high and low performing staff?

As classroom observations are collected throughout the year by lead teachers, administrators, and other evaluators, evidence is collected on what is happening in the classroom. Schools and classrooms that have high performing students can have their data compared to those who have low performing students. We can identify traits of high performing teachers and help those teachers facing challenges to grow professionally.

As discussed in previous chapters, there are always external factors that will affect the students and thus the scores. The focus of the data analysis for teacher growth and development needs to be on the traits of good instruction and student interaction that we can control.

Why not create a professional growth plan for every educator?

Since no two people are identical in their interests, skills, or knowledge, no single plan for professional growth will work for everyone. It is important to design an individual professional growth plan as a working document. This plan will serve as a road map to help guide, track, and review professional progress. Taking a thoughtful approach to professional growth provides benefits not only to the educator, but even more significantly, to the children they encounter daily. Both administrators and teachers will be engaged in professional growth as they pursue goals associated with quality improvement initiatives, observed areas of strength and weakness, and teacher effectiveness initiatives.

What if every administrator had access to up to the minute analytics on strengths and challenges of their staff?

As administrators strive to build community within their corporation and individual buildings, time management is crucial. Being available to support teachers and support staff is essential to this progression. Providing real-time data dashboards allows building and district administrators to focus on the day to day management of their buildings and provides collaboration and additional data to support every educator.

What do we need to support teachers and decrease the teacher attrition rate?

Finding that the teachers in our study who received consistent, targeted feedback and support were less likely to leave their current positions, we can conclude that this would decrease teacher turnover and attrition. We must identify early challenges beginning teachers face and give them targeted professional development opportunities and support to be successful. Data reported on teachers and administrators in their first five years of teaching or administration can drive programming at the teacher/administrator preparation program level. We must develop less than effective teachers and support their growth locally, as there may not be a qualified replacement.

PART III

CHAPTER 14

PRACTICE

This section of the book is intended to discuss the process of evaluating teachers. However, it is cautionary, as there is no one checklist of *how to* items when it comes to teacher evaluation. We will outline some best practices and points of consideration for those establishing or developing their teacher evaluation guidelines.

Terminology centering around teacher evaluation varies by state and even by district. We often hear administrators and teachers talk about observations, evaluations, short, long, mini, walkthroughs, etc. Let's begin with the terminology for observation and evaluation.

We sometimes think of any visit to our classrooms by an evaluator as an evaluation, when often, these are really observations. An observation is a visit of any length (walkthrough, short, or long) to take notes on what is going on in the classroom. An evaluation, by contrast, is the analysis of the compilation of this observational data, in conjunction with other documentation (lesson plans, etc.), to place a judgment of the teacher's overall performance. Some people equate the observation to qualitative data (scripting or note taking) and the evaluation to the quantitative domain (numerical).

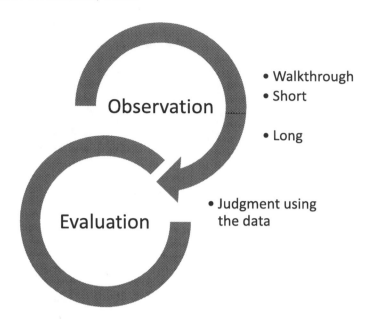

- Walkthrough
- Short

- Long

- Judgment using the data

Many schools are abandoning quick classroom checklists in favor of more comprehensive observations by both peers and administrators. As we have discussed, some of these changes have been mandated by legislation. However, teacher evaluations that rely on numerous highly structured classroom observations have become increasingly popular by all school systems. Some schools indicate that it has led to significant improvements in teacher performance (Taylor & Tyler, 2012). It is worth noting that this is not an either/or decision. Checklists, walkthroughs, and hall walks can provide beneficial supporting qualitative data to the comprehensive practice of teacher evaluation. It is when schools limit these to serve as the only indicator of teacher performance, and do not integrate them into an all-encompassing system of evaluation, that we limit the feedback and conversation essential to teacher growth and development.

On the following page is a sample flowchart for administrators implementing a teacher evaluation process. As always, district and state mandates may apply. Please ensure that you are following your individual district and state requirements.

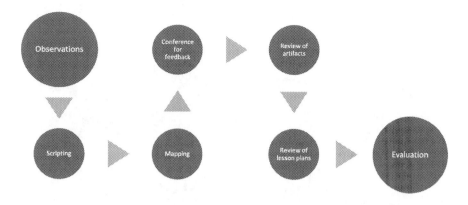

Of course, this is just a small portion of the cycle. As stated in previous chapters, observations are continuous and ongoing.

When conducting teacher performance evaluations, it is important to first determine what your district requires and values as good teaching. Regardless of these specific indicators, teachers and administrators must be engaged in its development to set the tone for growth and development. Teacher evaluations are a significant component of the administrator's management duties. To ensure that teachers are receptive to performance evaluations, encourage them to better engage in the practice by establishing expectations that encourage communication and allow teacher representatives to be part of the initial brainstorming sessions for rubric development. Encouraging this participation will set the tone that this is not a one-way dialogue, but collaboration that encourages self-assessment of their own performance.

Chapter Seven gave us an in-depth analysis of specific, actionable feedback. Dealing in generalities is not an effective way to get teachers to engage in their development. By being specific about the areas that need improvement, you can help teachers designate the areas that require progress and how the progress will be measured. Many teacher evaluation processes require teachers to set their professional goals based upon this feedback. After giving support for teachers to improve and meet their goals, administrators should continue observing to assess progress in these identified goal areas.

CHAPTER 15

CLASSROOM OBSERVATIONS

We begin our discussion of actual classroom observations with the scripting of evidence. This is the qualitative data gathering we have discussed in the previous chapter. Some think of this as notetaking, and that is a decent analogy. As we will discover in this chapter, there do exist some parameters for gathering strong evidence.

I always encourage evaluators to concentrate on improving teaching. When you enter the room, look at the culture of the room. Observe what the teacher is doing (that is why you are there!), but also what the students are doing. You might want to make a few quick notes about what is going on in the room, how many students there are, etc. This will not only serve as your first piece of scripting, but also a timestamp to document that the observation is beginning. Example:

"There are seventeen first graders in the room working on a math lesson".

This may not be anything that is rated, but it sets the tone for the beginning of the observation and documents that the evaluator is present in the room and beginning an observation. The evaluator may also wish to note if there is an instructional assistant in the room, along with any apparent elements of the climate and what is going on at the moment. Remember that as an evaluator, you are there to concentrate on assisting the teacher to improve and reflect. The observation is intended to provide targeted feedback to the teacher, and the teacher may devise their goals based upon this feedback.

Scripting

When we are conducting an observation, remember to write or script only what is seen, without judgment. Our judgment call will come later, when assigning a numerical value to the scripting based upon the rubric. Therefore, we are recording only the facts, or what we are observing during the visit. Our goal is to capture as much information during the observation as possible.

At a recent training of new evaluators, I was asked if it was necessary to get down everything the teacher or students said. My response was no, with a slight disclaimer. It is not intended, during scripting, for the evaluator to serve as a court reporter. Therefore, it is fine if all statements are not recorded. It is good practice to script some of the interactions between a teacher and students, as it is difficult for a teacher to dispute a direct quote.

My best example here is a personal one. I was once working with a teacher who had a tendency to be negative with her students. During an observation, I scripted the following:

"Teacher could be more positive in her interactions with students".

As an administrator and an evaluator, I felt this was a gentle and kind way to suggest that this teacher be more positive. But, as a teacher who was not aware of a problem with the way in which she interacted with students, it was a shock that came from nowhere. You see, I had witnessed multiple negative interactions between this teacher and her students. I had also fielded complaints from parents and other teachers about her negative attitude.

But to her, this was first. She did not see herself as a negative personality, and asked me for specific examples of how she had interacted in a less than positive manner with her students. I reviewed my scripting, and had nothing.

So what could I have done differently? This is a time when an exact conversation, listed in quotes, would have served both the teacher and evaluator well. By noting a specific example, I would have gathered better evidence. But more importantly, I could have provided this teacher with specific language upon which she could have improved. It would have been excellent feedback for her to actually see, word for word, what she was saying to students in her classroom.

DIANNA WHITLOCK, ED.D.

Evidence vs. Judgment

We all know that there is a difference between actual evidence and judgment. In fact, most curriculums require us to teach students to distinguish between *fact or opinion,* which requires a similar skill. Still, it is sometimes difficult for evaluators to remain in the mode of gathering evidence while observing lessons. As a result, we sometimes see statements such as the examples below appear in teacher evaluations:

Teacher is bad at classroom management.
Students are doing a great job.
Most students are on task and paying attention.

While the first two statements may be obvious to the evaluator who wrote them, there is no evidence present. These are entirely based upon opinion. The evaluator in this case must provide specific examples of what is going in the room in order for these to be evidence statements. For example, specific student behaviors that are disruptive or are in conflict with the school's behavior system would be acceptable evidence for the first statement on classroom management. In the second example, what about the students' behaviors or the teacher's instructional strategies compel the evaluator to say that they are doing a *great job*?

The third statement is better, as it does state what the students are doing (paying attention). However, the term *most* remains subjective. This is an example of an evidence statement that could be made stronger by stating how many students are on task and paying attention. A better, or stronger evidence statement might be:

6 students talking when teacher is giving directions.

Modifying this statement does two things. First, it tells the evaluator and the teacher specifically how many students are off-task. Secondly, it names the specific, observed off-task behavior of the students.

One of my favorite examples of a teacher utilizing specific scripting feedback comes from a first-grade classroom. I actually had a first-grade teacher utilize the scripting in her evaluation as a teachable moment for her students. While I was observing her classroom, I made note of the fact that while she was writing on the board and explaining a concept, five students were digging in their desks. She shared with me that she appreciated knowing this, and used it, in that wonderful way that first grade teachers everywhere possess, to discuss this with her students, by saying, "Now boys and girls, when Mrs. Whitlock visited yesterday, she saw five people digging in their art boxes during the lesson. We know that that is not what we are supposed to be doing during math time...".

Let me take a moment to clarify. I do not support a teacher utilizing any part of the evaluation process to reprimand or blame students. Nor do I support the teacher who threatens students prior to a planned observation visit by an evaluator. But I do feel that this teacher did an excellent job of taking the feedback provided in her evaluation and utilizing it to help her students realize the importance of student behaviors during instructional time. Delivery is key in this example.

Remember that it is also appropriate to record direct quotes during scripting. While you are not required to take down everything (remember that you are not a court reporter), this can provide good evidence in some cases. Let's look at another example:

T: *"Who is the main character in the story?". (1 second wait) "No one knows? It's Scout."*

This evidence statement can then be mapped to an indicator on wait time. In this example, it would be extremely beneficial for your teacher evaluation platform to contain a timestamp. If it does not, I highly recommend utilizing your phone or other device to document wait time and transition times. Teachers often do not realize the length of time they are giving students to answer, and this documentation provides excellent feedback. Another time that this might be useful:

Ten minutes to get out books and for teacher to begin lesson.
Students chose books in less than two minutes and returned to their seats.

This is valuable documentation for an indicator on maximizing instructional time. We may also want to list specific strategies employed by the teacher:

Teacher utilized 'turn and talk' and 'thumbs up/down' during lesson.

This may be helpful if there are school wide initiatives or if there has been a recent professional development on a specific instructional strategy.

Making Evidence Stronger

Let me share yet another example of a time when my scripting was less than perfect. (Yes, there are many!) I was evaluating in a primary classroom. A student was being somewhat disruptive. The teacher had the class begin an activity, then went over to the disruptive students' desk, kneeled down and whispered something to the student. The student then became compliant and re-directed. This was a perfectly appropriate interaction, to the best of my knowledge. My scripting for this was as follows:

Teacher handled discipline of students privately and appropriately.

While I do believe that this was true, the above is not a strong evidence statement. It is subjective in nature. Further, I really have no idea what the teacher said to the student! In hindsight, as an evaluator, I should have followed up with the teacher to find out what she said to the student. Not because I believed that she was saying anything inappropriate, but just to provide targeted feedback on the situation and confirm that what she did and said was effective in redirecting the students' behavior. This could be an excellent talking point during a post observation conference. But even as a secondary evaluator conducting a short observation, which often does not include a post conference, a better evidence statement might have been:

Teacher privately made a brief comment to student to re-direct off task-behavior.

This takes out the subjective word *appropriately* and gives a more detailed description of what is happening. Since we are often trying to get down as much evidence as possible, it is a good idea to check for weak evidence right after an observation, while the lesson is fresh in your mind. Best scenario for me has always been to go back to my office (or another quiet place) following an observation to clean up typos and check to see if my evidence statements could be strengthened. But as we all know, going back to the office can be detrimental to conducting observations, as it is so easy to get caught up in other responsibilities. If I am out doing observations in multiple classrooms, I try to do this clean-up check by the end of the day.

When I have been asked if scripting is just a fancy name for note-taking, again, I think that this is an appropriate analogy. The idea is to capture as much as possible without worrying about getting everything down. The best scripting is a balance of direct quotes between teacher and students and statements of what is going on overall in the classroom. Easy, right?

Mapping

After gathering information through scripting, the evaluator will begin mapping. This may be right after the clean-up of the scripting, and while the lesson is still fairly fresh in the evaluator's mind. After the scripting, the evaluator will need to look at the rubric and begin to *match* the scripting to indicators on the rubric. Mapping can be conducted in two different ways, or a combination of both. An evaluator may look at an indicator on the rubric and ask themselves if they saw evidence of this indicator in their scripting. Or, an evaluator may look at a piece of scripted evidence and ask themselves if it supports an indicator on the rubric. Most evaluators use a combination of the two methods.

For example, if there is an indicator on the rubric stating that the teacher uses checks for understanding before moving forward in the lesson, the evaluator may look through scripting statements and map the following statement to this indicator:

Teacher utilizes exit tickets to give to students when they answer correctly. Has students hold up tickets to assess if all students are understanding concept.

Likewise, if the evaluator has scripted that 17 of 20 students are on task and contributing to the discussion (hopefully with specific examples of student comments), this may be mapped to the following indicator:

At least ¾ of students are on task and engaged in the lesson.

Rubric Indicator   Scripting

| Teacher checks for understanding at pivotal moments of the lesson before moving forward with instruction | *Teacher utilizes exit tickets to give to students when they answer correctly. Has students hold up tickets to assess if all students are understanding concept.* |
| At least ¾ of students are on task and engaged in the lesson | *17 of 20 students are on task and contributing to the discussion.* |

It is worth noting that mapping is not always a one to one match. It is likely that one piece of evidence may meet multiple indicators on the rubric. This is especially true if an evaluator scripts long sentences or gives detailed descriptions. Likewise, several pieces of scripted evidence may meet the same indicator. This may be likely if a teacher is strong in a specific area; the evaluator may see multiple examples that support an indicator on the rubric.

Sometimes an evaluator, while mapping, will have a piece of evidence that they have scripted that does not match an indicator on the rubric. In essence, the evaluator has deemed the evidence important enough to script during the observation, but cannot find the perfect spot on the rubric that seems to be an appropriate match. Should the evaluator delete this piece of scripting, or leave it in? The final decision rests upon the professional judgment of the evaluator, but most times when I have this conversation with evaluators in trainings and consultations, the consensus is to leave the scripting in, unmapped. These comments can still serve as feedback and discussion points for the post conference conversation. If this is happening frequently, the evaluator may wish to discuss this with the rest of the administrative team. It is possible that this could lead to discussions on revision of the rubric to include the observed components.

Best practice dictates that when an evaluator is in the classroom for an observation, he or she should only be scripting, and save the mapping for later. That being said, the reality of the situation is that administrators are the ultimate multi-taskers. We all know that the busy administrator makes a daily practice of eating lunch, talking on the phone, and checking emails at the same time. Therefore, it is not unusual for an administrator to be tempted to map a piece of scripting while still conducting the observation. I think that this can be justified, particularly if a piece of evidence stands out as an obvious match to an indicator to be mapped, and the evaluator may want to make a note or go ahead and map so it isn't forgotten. The caution here is to not get so caught up in mapping that you miss other important elements of the lesson that may need to be scripted.

Rating

In addition to the matching of scripting to an indicator, most evaluation plans require an evaluator to assign a value from the rubric. Many of the rubrics discussed in Chapter Four are based upon a four-point scale, requiring the evaluator to mark a specific indicator as highly effective, effective, improvement necessary, or ineffective. While the language may vary, most rubrics are designed with something similar in terms of rating a piece of scripted evidence.

Watch for Missed Opportunities

Sometimes, the evaluator gets so involved on what is happening in the classroom, that it is easy to overlook what *should* be happening in the classroom. As we are recording the great traits of teaching, we should also be checking, during mapping, those indicators for which there is no evidence.

If there is no evidence to support an indicator on the rubric, the evaluator should ask if this particular indicator is not relevant to the lesson being observed, or if the teacher failed to do something that they should have. If the latter is the case, then the evaluator needs to look at the improvement necessary or ineffective categories to see if they are appropriate. If so, the evaluator can mark this and note that there was no evidence observed. For example, if throughout a long observation, which is typically 30 minutes or more in length, the evaluator does not witness any checks for understanding, this likely needs to be addressed. The evaluator should go to the section on the rubric that encompasses language on checking for understanding, and look at the needs improvement or ineffective categories for this indicator. Since there is no scripting to support this (since it was not observed), then there are two options for documentation. The first would be to add a sentence or two in the scripting section stating that checks for understanding were not present during the lesson, and map this to the appropriate category (needs improvement or ineffective). To make the evidence stronger, I have known evaluators to copy and paste the exact language on the rubric and place it in the scripting box, so the teacher can see exactly what is present on the rubric and not present in the observations. If the rubric states:

Teacher checks for understanding before moving ahead with instruction,

then the evaluator would copy this into the scripting, and perhaps add a few lines about how these checks were not observed during the lesson.

Artifacts

What do you consider an artifact? When I was first comprising slides to train administrators on artifact collection and approval, I started browsing for pictures to add to my slide deck. What kept appearing were pictures of museum collections of historical treasures. This is actually an applicable description of the artifact to represent good teaching. The idea of an artifact is to not only document, but to also showcase the elements of an employee's performance.

Interestingly enough, when I speak with educators about teacher evaluation, the area where I hear the most concerns (complaints?) is the gathering and storing of artifacts. I think that this is because it can be cumbersome and time consuming. If a district is not utilizing an online evaluation system, these may need to be compiled, stored, and rated on paper. Even if a district is utilizing a more technical system, the artifacts still need to be uploaded and rated.

But there is great value in the process. Have you ever had an evaluator leave your classroom and feel like he or she missed the best part of the lesson? Artifact sharing allows the teacher to share the *best part* with the evaluator at his or her own convenience. By uploading a lesson plan or pictures/video of a culminating student project, the teacher has the chance to ensure that the evaluator has a complete picture of the entire lesson and follow up activities.

Another valuable part of artifact collection is the reflection and conversations that can ensue during pre and post conferences. This might even spark feedback from the evaluator to the teacher for goal setting, professional development, and subsequent observations.

I cannot stress enough the importance of teachers collecting and uploading their own artifacts. Sometimes when working with administrators, I hear that they are gathering these for the teacher. This is troublesome to me for two reasons. First and foremost, it quickly becomes a time issue. The tasks of gathering and uploading artifacts for an entire staff, while also gathering and uploading for yourself, is colossal. (Yes, administrators need to gather these too; more on that later in the chapter!) But more importantly, if this is to be an exercise in reflection and self-improvement, it needs to be individual and personal. Teachers should be gathering samples of their practices and reflecting on ways in which they can improve and grow.

Another caution is to set the tone of gathering artifacts throughout the year. It is not as conducive to growth for a teacher or administrator to wait until May to upload their artifacts, or to create an artifact just for the sake of having enough artifacts. Administrators may wish to guide this by setting deadlines for artifact upload throughout the year, so it is a progressive, overall picture of a teacher's progress. Likewise, administrators should be evaluating and rating artifacts throughout the school year.

This provides feedback to teachers throughout the year so they can focus on growth and improvement prior to the last day of school. To help make the artifact practice less cumbersome for all, I also recommend setting parameters for the number of artifacts per teacher (minimum and maximum) in your district guidelines.

Rating Artifacts

As an evaluator, along with classroom visits, approving and rating artifacts is a crucial step in gathering evidence for effective feedback for teacher growth and development. It is also the only way in which to measure the domains of the teacher evaluation rubric that are not observable. Some of these may be domains measuring professionalism and leadership. These would require teachers to provide documentation for meeting the standard. The evaluator must then determine if the artifact does in fact meet the criteria for the standard, and rate the artifact based upon rubric criteria.

What Qualifies as an Artifact?

One of the most difficult components of artifact gathering and upload can be getting educators to showcase their best efforts. Educators tend to be extremely humble people by nature and may not be comfortable sharing their successes. Another source of concern for some teachers is that by documenting growth and improvement, we are asking them to take a risk by sharing their less than perfect experiences in the beginning of implementing a new lesson or strategy.

It may also take some guidance for administrators and teachers to determine what is appropriate when sharing artifacts. I have worked with teachers who were concerned with what was appropriate for documentation for the unobservable domains. This is particularly true of the domain representative of leadership. Often, teachers assume that leadership means a desire to progress into the administrative field. I have heard teachers say:

I don't have aspirations of becoming a lead teacher, department chair, or a building administrator. I love being a classroom teacher, and just want to improve at my craft. Will this hurt my score in the leadership domain?

While I think everyone agrees that it should not, this teacher may need some guidance in what teacher leadership can look like and some examples of activities that may be appropriate artifact documentation. Some examples are:

- Sharing new knowledge with peers
- Demonstration of school/community resources
- Newsletter/classroom webpage
- Supervision of student teacher/intern
- Parent/Teacher conference participation
- Professional development leader documents
- Coaching log
- Journal
- Committee participation
- Professional organizations
- Student appreciation letters
- Meeting minutes/documentation of meeting goals
- Parent communication log
- Professional development log
- Book Study Materials
- Action Research

This list is not all inclusive, but is intended to stimulate ideas for ways in which teachers can serve in leadership roles in their current instructional positions.

Administrator Artifacts

While this section has thus far focused on teacher artifacts to document their instructional practices and professional and leadership activities, do not forget that as an administrator, you will also be required to document your professional activities related to leadership. As with some of the teacher domains, most administrative standards are not observable. Therefore, it is essential to choose artifacts that represent your performance in each of the standards on the administrative evaluation rubric.

CHAPTER 16

CONFERENCES

We continue to focus on providing feedback as the cornerstone of teacher evaluation. Pre and post conferences are essential to making sure that this occurs. While best practice dictates that some type of conferences be a part of the overall evaluation practice, some districts have modified this to fit their individual needs. In this chapter, we will explore the purposes of both the pre and post conference, and recommendations for administrators to make these successful.

Pre-conference

The pre-conference, or planning conference, typically occurs prior to a planned, or formal observation. This is an appropriate time for the teacher and evaluator to discuss what will be happening during the upcoming classroom visit. Some of this may be included in the lesson plan, but it is still a good time to discuss in greater detail what the observer will see in terms of objectives, learning environment, and assessments. The teacher may also wish to share characteristics and behaviors of students that are expected during the lesson.

This is also a good time for the evaluator and teacher to review the rubric and what is expected for the performance indicators. Sometimes, evaluators and teachers limit the scope of the rubric and agree upon specific indicators for observation. One concern of this practice is that the evaluator may witness excellent examples of an indicator outside of this scope, and it would be beneficial for the evaluator and teacher to capture this. However, there is a place for this limitation of scope. If a teacher has struggled with a particular rubric indicator in a previous observation, the evaluator may have assigned a professional development task, with the understanding that they would return to re-evaluate that specific indicator in the future. Regardless of whether or not the administrator chooses to limit the scope, the pre-conference is the perfect time to discuss this with the teacher.

Some districts have elected to utilize a pre-conference form containing the key points listed above. This replaces the actual sit-down portion of the pre-conference, but still encourages the teacher to reflect upon goals and strategies. Likewise, the evaluator can prepare for the observation and know what to expect upon reading the form.

Post-conference

The post conference, also called a reflection conference, is crucial to effective teacher evaluation conversations. This is the main opportunity that exists to have conversation around what was observed in the classroom.

As educators, most of us were trained in some area of reflective practice, and were encouraged to assess situations and projects when completed to evaluate what went well, and what we can do better next time around. The post evaluation conference is the very crux of reflective practice in the teacher evaluation process! While scripted feedback is useful, sitting down with the teacher and discussing this scripted evidence, and how and why it relates to a specific rubric indicator, takes the discussion to the next level. Administrators can utilize this scripting to make conference conversations with teachers more purposeful, leading to improvement in their teaching strategies and overall craft (Baker, 2017).

Teachers may set their goals for improvement and growth during these conferences. Likewise, administrators may assign professional development tasks based upon the observation data, and the post conference is the place in which to discuss this. If a teacher is exceptional in a specific indicator, the administrator may take the time during the post conference to discuss how the teacher can mentor and guide peers to excel in this area.

While some districts are putting their pre-conference tasks into a form to gather information prior to an observation, this is usually not recommended for the post conference. The post conference sets the tone for a feedback rich culture in our schools and brands teacher evaluation as a method of teacher improvement and growth. Like so many other elements of teacher evaluation, conversation is the focus of the post conference.

In working with schools, I find that the post evaluation conference can be stressful for both the teacher and the evaluator. This may be true even if the teacher is not struggling. When a teacher is performing extremely well in the eyes of the evaluator, there is a temptation to finish the conference quickly, make a few positive comments and praises, and assume everything is OK. Remember when we discussed giving feedback to ALL teachers? This is the time! Again, much as teachers need to provide feedback and extended opportunities for their high performing students, as well as support to their low performing students, the high performing teacher still needs feedback. Further, this is an excellent opportunity to discuss with the high performing teacher how he or she may become a mentor to others, or perhaps conduct some action research on a topic of high performance. If we are truly encouraging a growth mindset in our schools, we must be prepared to support all of those around us to excel and improve.

For the struggling teacher, the conference can be even more stressful for both the teacher and evaluator. This may be the time to have some tough conversations on areas in which the teacher may improve. Again, preparation is imperative. To tell the struggling teacher that he or she is struggling, and not have a plan prepared for improvement, is in conflict with the growth mindset that you are trying to create in your school.

It is necessary to be clear to a struggling teacher that you have some legitimate concerns as a result of your observation. If you have created a culture of feedback, growth, and continuous improvement in your school, and if you can back up your concerns with documented, scripted evidence, then it is easier for the teacher to understand that your trepidation is based upon observed data and not personal judgment.

Conducting the Post Conference

When conducting the post conference, keep the focus on feedback and open dialogue. Some common reminders for the post conference are outlined below

1. Welcome teacher

As with any conference, we want to ensure that everyone is comfortable and that the atmosphere remains non-threatening. If you choose to meet in your office, you might want to consider the seating arrangement, and eliminate your desk as a barrier. It might make the teacher more comfortable to sit at a table or in chairs that have been place side by side. This is an excellent time to thank the teacher for letting you visit their classroom and name a few specific examples of what you enjoyed about the visit.

2. Set expectations

It is appropriate to review the purpose of the evaluation conference and what will be covered. Focus on sharing feedback and open dialogue.

3. Begin with positives

Even for a struggling teacher, there is always something positive with which to open the conference. This is highly recommended, as it can help set a positive tone for the conference.

4. Engage the teacher in conversation

The best conferences are a conversation, not a simple readback from the evaluator. Sometimes it can be difficult for the evaluator to engage the teacher. Therefore, some evaluators find success in utilizing the same questioning and listening techniques we utilize when questioning students, such as offering several correct answers, paraphrasing the teacher's comments, etc. This encourages collaboration, as well as self-assessment and reflection from the teacher. Often, evaluators will open with a question as simple as, *How do you think the lesson went?*

Conference for a Struggling Teacher

The most important point to remember when conferencing with a struggling teacher is that we are focusing on teacher growth and improvement. By encouraging the teacher to identify those elements of the observation that may need some work or the strategies for which they might need support, the desire to improve becomes internalized.

If the teacher does not identify areas for improvement, the evaluator may need to take the lead. It might be most productive to limit the areas for improvement to one or two. This keeps the overall tone positive and supportive, without overwhelming the teacher.

Depending upon the degree of self-awareness on the part of the teacher, the evaluator may need to utilize statements similar to the ones below to help them come to an understanding of their areas of needed improvement.

- *Tell me more about the different checks for understanding you used during your lesson and if you thought these were successful.*
- *I noticed that during the lesson, you re-explained the definition of "multiples", but 6 students were struggling with the assignment.*
- *I think that your students were having difficulty understanding the concept of multiples. An example of this was when…*

This is a good time for the evaluator to refer to the scripted evidence. By stating the documented, observed behavior of the teacher, there is no room for debate, and the focus can remain on improvement and growth. If a teacher does present a rationale to dispute the scripted piece of evidence, the evaluator should listen. Ultimately, it is the professional discretion of the evaluator that determines what to do with this scripting if the teacher takes issue with it and believes that the scripting is unfair or inappropriate. My go to response is usually to ask the teacher to upload an artifact to prove their rationale.

This is also the time to discuss the steps in which you will help the teacher improve, including specific strategies, timelines, and assessments.

The evaluator and teacher may set a time for a follow up observation to assess.

It is beneficial to know your staff well, including how they might respond to feedback. While some teachers are open to feedback and may even ask for ways in which they can improve, some teachers may be more sensitive or defensive about such commentary. This is where, once again, a culture of feedback and growth comes into play. The more that these become engrained in the culture of the school, the more receptive your teachers will be to the suggestions as part of the feedback process. Building strong relationships with your staff, especially those who may be easily intimidated by what they consider criticism, can be helpful to this culture as well.

Wrap-up

While the dialogue should have been continuous throughout the conference, the evaluator should always ask the teacher if there are any additional comments, questions, or concerns before concluding the conference. I also recommend ending with the following two questions:

- *How can I help you improve?*
- *What will you do to commit to change?*

This focuses on the sharing of suggestions for growth, as well as labels and reinforces some concrete strategies for accountability purposes. Above all, be sure to remain professional in your interactions and keep all conference dialogue positive and confidential.

CHAPTER 17

GROWTH PLANS

Since the focus of the evaluation process is growth, it should come as no surprise that we add a chapter on feasible growth plans. While some schools or districts may refer to these as professional development plans, there are a few differences. Usually, a growth plan refers to an individualized plan developed for a specific teacher, hopefully with input from that teacher. Think of the Individualized Education Plans (IEPs) that a school team creates to support a student. A professional development plan, by terminology, is usually the holistic plan to provide professional development and training to an entire school or district. In this chapter, we will look at how these two plans drive each other.

The National Comprehensive Center for Teacher Quality (NCCTQ) published a research and policy brief entitled *Linking Teacher Evaluation to Professional Development,* funded by the U.S. Department of Education. In that report, researchers concluded that (a) collected evidence of teacher performance should drive development strategies, and (b) the alignment between teacher evaluation and growth should begin with identifying sources of reliable evidence (NCCTQ, 2012). Among the chief thoughts, concerns, and best practices discussed by the authors of that report, were the following:

- No one performance metric can provide all the information needed to accurately assess a teacher's performance. Using multiple measures helps to understand the full range of a teacher's abilities, and to paint a more complete picture of their strengths and weaknesses. Triangulating results from various metrics also enables greater confidence in the final results when all scores are not in agreement.

- Teacher buy-in is the leading characteristic of high-quality professional development for teachers. The best scenarios occur when teachers are involved and contributing to professional development activities. Buy in is also essential; teachers must believe in the value of the professional development (NCCTQ, 2012).

- It's vital for teachers, evaluators, and leaders to be on the same page regarding expectations, including what is being observed and evaluated based upon the standards or indicators in the rubric (NCCTQ, 2012). It's the only way to drive out subjectivity, biases, ambiguity, and misunderstandings.

Growth and Professional Development Plans

A strong evaluation plan should drive professional growth of all employees in the school district, not just those in need of improvement. It is considered best practice to provide all teachers with professional development and growth (Indiana Department of Education, 2012). In addition, analysis of teacher evaluation data should drive school-wide and district-wide professional development opportunities. As funding for professional development becomes scarcer, it is necessary to target specific areas of need and make the most of those professional development dollars. This is easily done by targeting the specific strengths and challenges of individual buildings and even teachers in a district, then tailoring growth and development plans, as well as professional development initiatives, to specific needs of teachers.

If a school is utilizing a teacher evaluation management system, it is likely a little easier to track growth of individual teachers. But regardless of your method of managing data, an individual professional growth plan should be a working document to serve as a road map to help guide, track, and review professional progress. Taking this thoughtful approach to professional growth provides benefits not only to the educator, but to the children they instruct each day.

Another advantageous element of a management tool is that it encourages engagement of both the administrator and teacher in developing plans for professional growth as they pursue goals associated with the quality of improvement initiatives, observed areas of strength and weakness, and teacher effectiveness initiatives.

Collected teacher evaluation data can, and should, be used to drive professional development. Collected analytics provide insight on teacher development needs. This is true if the analyzed data applies to all educators in a district or building, a specified group, or an individual. Some districts are implementing professional development tasks directly into their evaluation management portals, to provide immediate, targeted professional development. By creating this culture of continuous learning, teachers and school districts can make better use of time and financial resources and promote teacher retention and growth.

This seems an appropriate place to point out that while growth plans are usually used for struggling teachers, they may also have a place for other teachers. While we all strive to hire the best teachers, some that we have *inherited* may need some extra support and guidance. Likewise, a new hire may have excellent strengths in some areas of instruction, but may need support in other targeted areas. With new methods of data collection for teacher candidates, an administrator may be able to view these areas for improvement, and immediately begin discussing plans for targeted professional growth.

Creating Professional Growth Plans

We know that keeping teachers motivated ensures education performance at optimal levels in your school or district. Therefore, it is critical to focus on those efforts that keep teachers actively engaged in their own professional growth.

Professional growth plan development, which has been used in numerous corporations, can give employees more ownership in their own evaluations and performance reviews. If used effectively, you can get more mileage out of your teacher evaluation data. Take a look at the tips below for engaging teachers through professional growth plans.

1. **Set expectations beforehand.** Don't wait until two to three months into the school year to finally communicate the expectations you have for teachers' overall performance. Be specific about your expectations, outlining the areas that are of utmost importance to you. Those expectations could include training, taking courses, communicating with parents, and helping to improve student test scores.

2. **Provide feedback throughout the school year.** Once again, feedback is key! Just as you shouldn't wait to outline expectations, don't wait until the end of the year to finally get around to checking performance. Give teachers the opportunity to improve their performance by providing regular feedback throughout the school year. If necessary, schedule that time to gauge how the teachers are performing. Appoint peer teachers to observe the teachers to supplement that feedback.

3. **Make sure the goals are backed by actions.** When helping teachers outline their goals, make sure they are developing a plan of action to accomplish them. This amplifies their ownership in the improvement process. For example, if the goal is to help students improve their writing skills with essays, have the teacher help determine how those improvements will be measured as well as the lesson plans, tutoring and observations needed to accomplish it. Make sure you put those details in writing. The post conference is an excellent time to discuss these actions, based upon the observation data. You will also need to provide resources to support the goal.

4. **Implement a strategy to monitor progress.** To ensure a comprehensive approach to your teacher evaluation, make sure that you have a system in place to easily monitor notes and feedback on progress. It is vital to your team's ability to follow through. Follow up observations, with the identified areas of growth at the forefront, should be a part of this progress monitoring. Be sure to acknowledge successes along the way.

The professional growth plan, or PGP, serves as a proactive means of collaboration between administrators and teachers to develop a detailed plan for improvement, based upon observed data. The goal is improved teaching and quality instruction (Freeman, 2013).

As with other elements of the evaluation process, it is important that a growth plan not be viewed as a punishment, but rather an exercise in growth and development. Providing opportunities for teacher collaboration and input when designing the plan will assist in this being viewed as part of the culture of feedback and improvement you are creating in your school.

CHAPTER 18

FINALIZATIONS

With data collected, conferences conducted, and feedback given throughout the year, the time will come for the administrator to make a judgement based upon evidence, or a finalization. The finalization is the analysis of all data to assign a final rating, or ranking, for an individual teacher. This final ranking is usually assigned by the building administrator, using data from not only their observations, but all secondary evaluators who have gathered observational data.

It is crucial to realize that in many cases, this final rating score is all that district level administrators, school board members, and state legislative bodies see in regard to teacher evaluation. Therefore, it is vital that administrators are encompassing all collected data when assigning this final score. While we encourage all parties involved in teacher evaluation to drill down the data and analyze the specific areas of strengths and challenges of teachers, this is often not a required reporting component.

An Average, or a Progression?

When working with schools on their evaluation process, I often am asked if our evaluation platform will average the data, giving the administrator a final number, and therefore eliminating even more guesswork or subjectivity. At first examination, this seems like a perfect solution. But upon closer examination, this may not be what we want to support a culture of growth. Let's look at a hypothetical example of assigning finalizations.

A school has conducted all observations, approved artifacts, conducted pre and post conferences, set goals for teacher professional development, and is now ready to assign teachers a final number reflective of their yearly performance. Principal Sky, who is the primary evaluator, has ensured that all observational data has been entered into the management system, and as a result has a numerical average for each teacher. Principal Sky sits down after school one afternoon to look at the ratings for two of his struggling teachers, Miss Sunshine and Mr. Moon, who have both received an average score of *2,* placing them in the *Improvement Needed* category, per the district's rubric.

Upon closer examination, Principal Sky finds that observations for Miss Sunshine have been marked consistently by multiple evaluators as mostly *2*'s throughout the year. Miss Sunshine has also not submitted many artifacts supporting her professional development or growth throughout the year. For these reasons, Principal Sky feels that her average rating is fair and reflective of a rating of *Improvement Needed* for a final rating, represented by a *2.*

Principal Sky then looks at the data for Mr. Moon. Mr. Moon began the school year with observation data of *2*'s, (representative of *Improvement Needed*), and even a few *1*'s (*Ineffective*). Throughout pre and post conferences, Mr. Moon communicated with his evaluators, set goals for improvement, and documented completion of multiple professional development opportunities. When a secondary evaluator conducted a follow up observation of Mr. Moon in November, focusing on identified areas for improvement, Mr. Moon implemented the strategies from the professional development activities, and his scores in these areas increased. During the second semester, Principal Sky assigned a veteran teacher to mentor Mr. Moon, who continued to document professional development and meetings and observations by his mentor teacher. By the spring of the school year, Mr. Moon was receiving observation marks consisting of *2*'s (*Improvement Needed*) and *3*'s (*Effective*).

Mathematically, the two teachers both received an average score of 2. However, which teacher showed growth and improvement? Most would agree that in a culture of growth, Mr. Moon would deserve the

3, because that is the number he achieved after support and guidance from administrators and a mentor teacher. If we are effectively measuring growth, we should rate teachers where they are at the end of the school year. To take this one step further, Principal Sky should be documenting what supports were offered or assigned to both Miss Sunshine and Mr. Moon, to justify the difference in final ratings.

After taking through this type of an example, most administrators change their minds about the averages, and wish to keep their professional judgment at the forefront of finalizations. The downside is that it is more subjective, but if administrators are appropriately trained in the evaluation process and analysis of evaluation data, then they are more than qualified to assign a final score based upon this data. Most importantly, they are placing emphasis on the growth and improvement element of teacher evaluation and creating a culture of feedback and continuous development in their schools.

Some schools still choose to average, and this is not an incorrect philosophy to adopt. Local control drives these decisions, and the culture of the district may dictate that this is the method favored by teachers and administrators. In fact, some teachers prefer the system of averages, because they are not comfortable in allowing administrators the subjectivity to override a final average. Teachers may also be more comfortable with the averaging method because it is how we assess students with traditional grades. Administrators may prefer to take the subjectivity out of the finalizations, thus placing more responsibility on the numbers in the system, and not on their personal judgment. This is one more element of teacher evaluation that will need to be discussed and weighed as polices and plans are determined.

CHAPTER 19

CONCLUSION

We have discussed a number of elements of teacher evaluation. The takeaway is that it is a practice of growth and development, not a punitive measure to try to *catch* someone doing the wrong thing.

As our educational workforce changes, the next generation of teachers and administrators continue to need consistent, targeted feedback in order to develop professionally. If done intentionally, teacher evaluation practice can serve as a guiding force in this development.

Establishing and nurturing your district's evaluation process may seem like a task for another day, but in reality, it deserves priority. It can help create a culture of communication, feedback, and professional practice that can drive your staff to an improved culture of collaboration and a growth mindset. As educational leaders, we all share a responsibility to create this culture and guide those around us. My hope is that this book inspires others to prioritize this mindset and develop the next generation of educational leaders.

One of the most relevant educational quotes in regard to teacher evaluation and development follows:

> *"If someone is going down the wrong road, he doesn't need motivation to speed him up. What he needs is education to turn him around." – Jim Rohn*

(as cited by Juma, 2019).

I hope that as educational leaders, we can continue to guide others down the right road.

REFERENCES

Andrews, K. (2016). *New Trends in the Evaluation of School Principals*, [Powerpoint slides]. Lecture at the National Summit for Principal Supervisors, Ft. Lauderdale, FL.

Baker, S. (2017). Evaluation of teachers—A principal's view [Blog post]. Retrieved from: https://www.standardforsuccess.com/ evaluation-of-teachers-a-principals-view/

Bartz, D., Thompson, K., & Rice, P. (2017). Enhancing the Effectiveness of Millennial Teachers Through Principals Using Performance Management. *National Forum of Educational Administration and Supervision Journal, 35 (4).*

Bersin, J. (2013). Time to scrap performance appraisals? *Forbes/Leadership.* Retrieved from: www.forbes.com

Buddin, R., & Croft, M. (September 2014). Recent Validity for Value-Added Measures of Teacher Performance. *ACT Research & Policy Issue Brief.* Retrieved from: http://forms.act.org/research/policymakers/pdf/ Measures-of-Teacher-Performance.pdf

Carver-Thomas, & Darling Hammond. (August 2017). Teacher turnover: Why it matters and what we can do about it. *Learning Policy Institute.* Retrieved from: https://learningpolicyinstitute.org/sites/default/files/ product-files/Teacher_Turnover_REPORT.pdf

Cooper, B., Fusarelli, L., & Randall, E. (2004). *Better policies, better schools: theories and applications.* Boston: Pearson, Allyn & Bacon.

Cydcor. (2018). 6 mistakes to avoid when giving feedback. Retrieved from: https://www.cydcor.com/blog/2018/03/6-mistakes-to-avoid-when-giving-feedback/

Danielson, C. (2007) *Enhancing professional practice.* Alexandria, VA: ASCD.

Danielson Group, The. (2013). Excerpt from the framework for teaching evaluation instrument. Retrieved from: https://www.ode.state.or.us/wma/teachlearn/commoncore/danielson-2013-rubric-only.pdf

Darling-Hammond, L., Amrein-Beardsley, A., Haertel, E., & Rothstein, J. (2012). Evaluating teacher evaluation. *Phi Delta Kappan*, 93(6), 8-15.

David, J. (2010, May). What research says about using value-added measures to evaluate teachers. *Association for Supervision and Curriculum Development*, 67(8), 81-82.

Drucker, P. (1954). *The Practice of Management*. New York, NY: Harper and Row.

Florida Department of Education. (n.d.). Retrieved from www.fldoe.org

Freeman, K. (2013, February 27). Professional growth plans...a win/win scenario [Blog post]. Retrieved from: https://www.standardforsuccess.com/professional-growth-plans-a-winwin-scenario/

Gallup, Inc. (2013). *The state of the American workplace report.* Retrieved from: https://www.gallup.com/services/176708/state-american-workplace.aspx

Gallup, Inc. (2016). *How millennials want to work and live. The six big changes leaders have to make.* Washington, D.C.

Gershon, L. (2015, May 12). A short history of standardized tests. *JSTOR Daily*. Retrieved from: https://daily.jstor.org/short-history-standardized-tests/

Greenleaf, R. (2002). *Servant leadership*: *A journey into the nature of legitimate power and greatness*. (25th anniversary edition) Mahwah: Paulist Press.

Halford, S. (April 7, 2011). Five steps for giving productive feedback. Retrieved from: www.entrepreneur.com/article/219437

Hanushek, E., & Rivkin, G. (2010). Using value-added measures of teacher quality. *National Center for Analysis of Longitudinal Data in Education Research*. Retrieved from: https://files.eric.ed.gov/fulltext/ED509683.pdf

Hollingworth, L. (2012). Why leadership matters: Empowering teachers to implement formative assessment. *Journal of Educational Administration*, 50(3), 365-379. Retrieved from: doi:http://dx.doi.org.ocproxy.palni.edu/10.1108/09578231211223356

Indiana Department of Education (n.d.). Retrieved from: www.doe.in.gov

Indiana Department of Education. (January 2012). *Equitable distribution of qualified, experienced teachers state plan.* Retrieved from www.idoe. in.gov.

Indiana Department of Education (2017). *Staff performance evaluation results.* Retrieved from: https://www.in.gov/sboe/2746.htm

Juma, N. (2019). 110 quotes about education and the power of learning. Retrieved from: https://everydaypower.com/quotes-about-education/

Kotter, J. (2008). *A sense of urgency.* [Kindle fire version]. Retrieved from Amazon.com

Marzano, R. J. (2012). The Two Purposes of Teacher Evaluation. *Educational Leadership*, 70(3), 14-19.

Merriam-Webster's dictionary. (2019). Retrieved from https://www. merriam-webster.com/dictionary/rubric.

National Comprehensive Center for Teacher Quality. (2012). Linking teacher evaluation to professional development: Focusing on improving teaching and learning. Retrieved from: https://gtlcenter.org/sites/ default/files/docs/LinkingTeacherEval.pdf

National Institute for Excellence in Teaching. (2010). TAP evaluation and compensation guide. Retrieved from: https://www.gpisd.org/ cms/lib01/TX01001872/Centricity/Domain/6651/TEC%20%20 handbook.pdf

National Policy Board for Educational Administration. (2011). Educational Leadership Program Standards. Retrieved from http://npbea.org/wp-content/uploads/2019/01/ELCC-Building-Level-Standards-2011.pdf

Oschner, K. (November 2010). Lecture at the NeuroLeadership Summit, Boston, MA.

Palestini, R. (2011). *Educational administration: leading with mind and heart.* (3rd ed.). Lanham, MD: Scarecrow Press.

Popham, W. J., & DeSander, M. (2014). Will the Courts Save Teachers?. *Educational Leadership*, 71(5), 55-58.

Pozen, R. (2013). The delicate art of giving feedback. *Harvard Business Review.* Retrieved from: https://hbr.org/2013/03/the-delicate-art-of-giving-fee

Redding, C. (2018). Teacher turnover is a problem-here's how to fix it. Retrieved from: https://theconversation.com/ teacher-turnover-is-a-problem-heres-how-to-fix-it-101584

Reform Support Network. (n.d.). Targeting Growth, Using Student Learning Objectives as a Measure of Educator Effectiveness. Retrieved from: https://www2.ed.gov/about/inits/ed/implementation-support-unit/tech-assist/targeting-growth.pdf

RISE Evaluation and Development. (n.d.). Retrieved from: www.riseindiana.org

Room 241 Team, The, (2012, October 31). Overview of Robert Marzano's model of teaching effectiveness [Blog post]. Retrieved from: https://education.cu-portland.edu/blog/classroom-resources/overview-of-robert-marzanos-model-of-teaching-effectiveness/

Silver Strong & Associates. (2013). Retrieved from https://thoughtfulclassroom.com/educator-effectiveness-and-evaluation/

Skourdoumbis, A. (2013). The (mis)identification of ineffective classroom teaching practice: critical interrogations of classroom teacher effectiveness research. *Asia-Pacific Journal of Teacher Education*, 41(4), 350-362. doi:10.1080/1359866X.2013.787393

Soslau, E., & Lewis, K. (2014). Leveraging Data Sampling and Practical Knowledge: Field Instructors' Perceptions About Inter-Rater Reliability Data. *Action in Teacher Education (Association of Teacher Educators)*, 36(1), 20-44.

Steele, J. Hamilton, L., & Stecher,B. (2011). Using student performance to evaluate teachers. *RAND Corporation*. Retrieved from: https://www.rand.org/pubs/research_briefs/RB9569.html

Stratford, M. (2016). The coming teacher shortage crisis. *Politico morning education*. Retrieved from: https://www.politico.com/tipsheets/morning-education/2016/09/the-coming-teacher-shortage-crisis-216339

Survey Data. (2016). *Unpublished raw survey data*. Available from Standard for Success.

Taylor, S., & Tyler, J. (2012). Can teacher evaluation improve teaching? *EducationNext*. Retrieved from: https://www.educationnext.org/can-teacher-evaluation-improve-teaching/

Tuman, L. (2016). Teacher evaluations in Georgia will focus less on student test scores. *News 12 NBC 26*. Retrieved from: https://www.wrdw.com/content/news/Teacher-evaluations-in-Georgia-will-focus-less-on-student-test-scores-386899131.html

US Department of Education. (July 2015). *Alternative student growth measures for teacher evaluation: Implementation experiences of early adopting districts.* (National Center for Education Evaluation and Regional Assistance, Institute of Education Sciences). Retrieved from:_https://ies.ed.gov/ncee/edlabs/regions/midatlantic/pdf/REL_2015093.pdf

Volmer, J. (2011). The Blueberry Story: The teacher gives the businessman a lesson. *NebraskaMATH.* Retrieved from: https://newsroom.unl.edu/announce/csmce/755/3329

Whitlock, D. (2016). *The State of Teacher Evaluation in Indiana.* Unpublished manuscript, Standard For Success, Cloverdale, IN.

Whitlock, T. (2015). When Incentives Harm Performance, What Scientists Know That Schools Don't. *SEEN, Southeast Education Network*, v. 17.2, pp. 72-75.

Whitlock, T. (2017). Student growth still a critical factor in teacher evaluation [Blog post]. Retrieved from: https://www.standardforsuccess. com/?s=Student+Growth+Still+a+Critical+Factor+in+Teacher+Evaluations&submit=

Wise Old Sayings, Words to live by (n.d.) Retrieved from https://www. wiseoldsayings.com/continuous-improvement-quotes/

Zenger, J., & Folkman, J. (2014). Your employees want the negative feedback you hate to give. *Harvard Business Review.* Retrieved from: https://hbr.org/2014/01/your-employees-want-the-negative-feedback-you-hate-to-give

Printed in the United States
By Bookmasters